WHO KILLED
the AVRO
ARROW?

Chris Gainor

FOLK
LORE
PUBLISHING

The Publisher: Folklore Publishing
Website: www.folklorepublishing.com

Library and Archives Canada Cataloguing in Publication

Gainor, Chris
    Who killed the Avro Arrow? / Chris Gainor.

Includes bibliographical references.
ISBN-13: 978-1-894864-68-8
ISBN-10: 1-894864-68-9

    1. Avro Arrow (Turbojet fighter plane) 2. Canada—Politics and government—
1957–1963. I. Title.

TL685.3.G22 2007   623.74'640971   C2007-904216-3

Project Director: Faye Boer
Project Editor: Wendy Pirk
Production: Jodene Draven
Cover Image: Courtesy of the Canada Aviation Museum, Ottawa.
Photography credits: Every effort has been made to accurately credit the sources
of photographs. Any errors or omissions should be reported directly to the
publisher for correction in future editions. Photographs courtesy of Avro
Museum (p. 75); Arthur Chamberlin (p. 193); Department of National Defence
(p. 9, p. 33, p. 80, p. 99, p. 214); Chris Gainor (p. 211); Wikipedia (p. 13, p. 73,
p. 83, p. 149, p. 155, p. 177)

We acknowledge the financial support of the Alberta Foundation for the Arts
for our publishing program.

We acknowledge the financial support of the Government of Canada through
the Book Publishing Industry Development Program for our publishing
activities.

PC: P5

Canadian   Patrimoine
Heritage   canadien

Dedication

THIS BOOK IS DEDICATED to my parents, Don and Toni Gainor, who, like the people of Avro Canada, grew up in a time of Depression and war and made the best of the challenges they faced in the second half of the 20th century.

Acknowledgements

I OWE MANY PEOPLE THANKS, including my faculty advisor at the University of Alberta, Dr. Robert W. Smith; Dr. Tom Saunders of the history department at the University of Victoria; Rolf Maurer, who gave me my first Arrow book all those years ago; and Tom Sheppard and Diane Dupuis, who helped me with my research in Ottawa.

I also want to thank Brian Lam, Barry Shanko, Ken Harman, Steve Pacholuk and my brother, Tim Gainor. My wife Audrey McClellan provided assistance in countless ways.

My interest in the Avro Arrow began by meeting some of the talented people who designed and built it, and I want to thank all the great people from Avro Canada I met over the past 13 years, some of whom are listed in the sources. While they will not necessarily agree with the conclusions I reach in this book, which are mine alone, my respect for them and their work remains undiminished.

Contents

Introduction

ON FEBRUARY 20, 1959, the Canadian government cancelled the CF-105 Avro Arrow program. In the nearly
half century that has since gone by, that day has
become known to many as "Black Friday," the day
that much more than an aircraft met its fate. To the
legions of Canadians who saw the Arrow as a symbol
of Canadian excellence, Black Friday marked the end
of an era in which Canadians thought they could do
anything—an era that began in World War II, when
Canada played a key role in the alliance that defeated
Nazi Germany and the Japanese Empire. Canadians
distinguished themselves on the battlefield as they
had done in World War I, and Canadians back at
home made their country an industrial colossus by
building the tanks, ships, aircraft and ammunition
that played a critical part in winning the war.

Canada's economy had historically been based on
resource extraction. By becoming the fourth-largest
supplier of arms to the Allies in World War II—only
the United States, the Soviet Union and Great Britain
built more weapons—Canada appeared to be joining
the ranks of major industrial powers, and Canadians
hoped to become much more than hewers of wood
and drawers of water. As the victorious wartime alliance broke up, and Canada, Britain, the U.S. and
Western European countries faced off against the
Soviet Union and its unwilling Eastern European

satellites, Canada's military and industry faced new challenges.

Many of the hopes that Canadians held in the Cold War were invested in the Arrow, and many people saw the demise of the Arrow as a turning point where Canada faced the limits of its economic power and political influence in the turbulence of the 1960s and the years that followed.

Today many Canadians, including large numbers who were born since the Arrow died, still debate how and why the project was cancelled. The Arrow has become the object of a great national myth about what might have been. Only five of the aircraft ever flew, and the fact that they were destroyed has sharpened the controversy. The remaining relics of the Arrow are now exhibited in museums, and the Arrow has become the object of many books, articles, souvenirs, documentaries, novels, plays and, most memorably, a television mini-series.

The Arrow was designed to defend Canada against a particular threat—Soviet bombers. Along the way, the Arrow became a symbol of Canada's hopes. The story of the Arrow touches on matters of military strategy, technological changes, economic strength, political leadership, Canada's relationship with the United States and Canada's place in the world. With all these factors affecting the fate of the Arrow, there are naturally many theories about why the Arrow was cancelled and where the responsibility lies for that decision. These theories arose from the people who built the Arrow, and from those who looked on and came to admire the aircraft. Like any large project of this type, the Arrow also drew a large number of critics, and their voices helped shape the dialogue about the aircraft and the legend that arose after its demise.

The Arrow marked a major milestone in the nearly 100 years of powered flight in Canada, and its echoes have reverberated to the present day. The story of the Avro Arrow began with the hopeful and exciting first days of aviation in Canada early in the 20th century.

~ 𝕏 ~

PART 1:

The Story of the Arrow

CHAPTER 1

Canada's Aviation Industry

CANADA'S FIRST SUCCESSFUL EFFORT to build and fly aircraft was a joint effort with the U.S. The Aerial Experiment Association was formed in Halifax on October 1, 1907, less than four years after Orville and Wilbur Wright made their historic first powered flight in North Carolina on December 17, 1903. The association was led by Alexander Graham Bell, the famous inventor who lived in both the U.S. and Canada. It included two Canadians, John A.D. McCurdy and Frederick W. "Casey" Baldwin, both of whom were engineering graduates from the University of Toronto, as well as two Americans, an engine builder from Hammondsport, New York, named Glenn H. Curtiss and Lieutenant Thomas H. Selfridge of the U.S. Army.

The group set to work experimenting with gliders and building aircraft, and on March 12, 1908, Baldwin became the first Canadian to fly a powered aircraft when he took to the air in the *Red Wing* at Hammondsport. McCurdy also flew that year, including a flight in the *Silver Dart*. The aircraft was shipped to Bell's summer home at Baddeck on Cape Breton Island, and on February 23, 1909, McCurdy made the first powered aircraft flight in Canada and the British

Empire when he flew the *Silver Dart* from the ice that covered Bras d'Or Lake.

The association disbanded shortly after that flight, and Curtiss went on to become a major aircraft manufacturer in the U.S. and a principal competitor of the Wright Brothers. Baldwin and McCurdy set up Canada's first aircraft manufacturing firm, the Canadian Aerodrome Company. Although their venture didn't last long, McCurdy and others established new companies to build aircraft in Canada.

The airplane proved its usefulness in World War I, and scores of Canadian pilots, such as Billy Bishop and Billy Barker, distinguished themselves in the fight as part of the British forces. The 1920s saw the establishment of the Royal Canadian Air Force (RCAF) and the creation of new aircraft builders and small airlines in Canada. Two of the biggest names in the Canadian aircraft business—de Havilland Canada in Toronto and Canadian Vickers, later known as Canadair, in Montreal—got their starts in the 1920s as offshoots of British companies. Many of Canada's former World War I pilots returned home to become bush pilots, opening up Canada's north. It was only in 1937 that the Canadian government formed Trans-Canada Air Lines (TCA), which became Air Canada in the 1960s. The company remained under government ownership until 1989.

The Depression years of the 1930s proved difficult for Canada's aircraft industry. In 1933, no aircraft were produced in Canada, but by 1938, the number had risen to 282, most of them going to the RCAF. That year, Canada had 12 aircraft firms.

The outbreak of World War II led to major changes in Canada's tiny aircraft industry. Great Britain needed aircraft built in a country that could obtain its own resources to build them and that was out of range of German bombs, and it needed outside help to train pilots to help fight the war. Britain looked to Canada, the senior member of the British Empire that was on its way to independence as a member of the British Commonwealth.

Once the war began in 1939, Canada's Liberal government under Prime Minister William Lyon Mackenzie King moved to expand Canada's armaments production, including aircraft. One of King's most powerful ministers was Clarence Decatur (C.D.) Howe, the dynamic American-born engineer who headed up the Department of Munitions and Supply. Educated at the Massachusetts Institute of Technology (MIT), Howe taught engineering there and at Dalhousie University before he moved to the Lakehead and became well known for building grain storage facilities. In 1935, he was elected to Parliament and immediately joined King's Cabinet, where he again proved his ability as a manager. By the time the war began, Howe was known as the "Minister of Everything." Howe had hired prominent business people and younger managers to run the vast wartime enterprises that had made Canada one of the world's great industrial powers during the war. These people, who the government paid a dollar a year while

C.D. Howe

~~∞⟨⟩∞~~

the businesses they had temporarily left covered their salaries, helped make Canada a major industrial power. After the war, most of the "dollar-a-year men" (almost none were women) formed the elite of the Canadian business community.

During World War II, more than 16,000 aircraft rolled out of Canadian plants. The overwhelming majority of those aircraft were designed in Britain and built in Canada under special wartime arrangements. Many of the aircraft were trainers used to support the British Commonwealth Air Training Plan, which trained 131,553 aircrew personnel, more than half of them for the RCAF.

As war clouds were gathering in 1938 and the British and Canadian governments began thinking about gearing up for war, the National Steel Car Corporation, a Hamilton-based rolling stock company, got a contract from the Canadian government to build Westland Lysander aircraft. The company built a small plant in the town of Malton, Ontario, next to a new airport that served the nearby city of Toronto. After the war broke out in 1939, National Steel Car expanded the Malton plant and made more Lysander aircraft, which were used by the British Army for spotting, dropping and retrieving agents behind enemy lines. The plant was also used to make more than 700 Avro Anson aircraft, which were used as trainers for multi-engine aircraft. Soon the Malton plant was turning out parts for Hampden bombers.

In 1942, the British wanted to dedicate National Steel Car to the Avro Lancaster bomber to fill a shortage in heavy bombers, but the firm was experiencing management problems after the death of its president. So in November of that year, the Canadian government nationalized the Malton plant, and it formed Victory Aircraft Ltd. to supervise production of the Lancasters for use by the Royal Air Force (RAF) in its bombing campaigns over Germany. By war's end, Victory Aircraft had produced 422 of the four-engine Lancasters at Malton.

The Lancaster work made Victory Aircraft the largest aircraft manufacturer in Canada during the war, with nearly 10,000 employees on the payroll in a plant that grew to more than 90,000 square metres. But even as the first Lancasters were rolling onto the tarmac at Malton, Canadian military and business leaders were already beginning to think about what would happen to the country's industrial capacity once the war was over. The years following World War I had proven difficult for the Canadian economy, and World War II was much bigger. While fear of economic dislocation drove their thoughts, so did the hope that the successes of wartime production would lead to new opportunities for Canadian business and workers. Outsiders, too, were impressed by what they saw in Canada during the war, and they saw the potential for profit.

Two leading figures at Hawker Siddeley Aircraft, which controlled most of Britain's aircraft production, came to Canada in 1943 to see its aircraft industry. Sir Frank Spriggs, the managing director of the company, and Sir Roy Dobson, managing director of the A.V. Roe Company, the Hawker Siddeley subsidiary that had developed the Anson and the Lancaster, were most impressed by what they found.

"If these so-and-so's can do this during a war, what can't they do after?" Dobson thought to himself.

During the trip, Spriggs and Dobson talked to Howe and other Canadian leaders about the potential of the Canadian aircraft industry. No plans or commitments were made, but people on both sides of the Atlantic were starting to think about how to keep Canada's aircraft production lines going after the war ended.

CHAPTER 2

The Birth of Avro Canada

THE FIRM THAT BECAME KNOWN as Avro Canada owes its existence to two unusual personalities who came together at the end of World War II—C.D. Howe and Sir Roy Dobson. While Howe wanted to keep at least some of Canada's aircraft business going after the war, he was determined to have it run by private business rather than the government.

In Dobson, the blunt-spoken and hard-driving Howe found someone he could deal with. In 1914, the Yorkshire-bred Dobson joined the aircraft company in Manchester started by Alliott Verdon Roe, the British aviation pioneer. Dobson quickly demonstrated his technical and entrepreneurial ability, and he soon moved into the management of the growing firm. After Roe sold the firm in a round of consolidations in the British aircraft industry between the wars, Dobson was put in charge and played key roles in developing and building aircraft such as the Anson. A man of immense charm, Dobson could summon great bluster when it was needed. He worked with famed aircraft designer Roy Chadwick to develop the Lancaster, creating the aircraft in defiance of instructions from the British government. The Lancaster went on to be credited with playing a key role in winning World War II in Europe.

Early in 1945, Howe began winding down production at Victory Aircraft and other enterprises under his control in anticipation of the end of the war. Dobson was visiting Canada regularly during this time. He spent time with the directors of Victory Aircraft and with Howe, and in June, his discussions with them led to a handshake arrangement for the takeover of the firm. According to Dobson, he and Howe agreed to a rent-purchase arrangement in which Hawker Siddeley would take over Victory Aircraft. "We were to pay half our profits in rent. But no profits, no rent," Dobson said. Because Britain's economy had been nearly bled dry by the war, no one could export currency from Britain at the time, so the new venture would need to marry Hawker Siddeley's expertise to Canadian capital and a Canadian workforce.

On the same visit to Canada, Dobson met one of Howe's dollar-a-year men, whom he befriended and offered a job with his new Canadian concern. Fred Smye, a 29-year-old who had proven himself as a manager in Howe's aircraft enterprises, accepted the offer and became the first employee of the new firm, which faced a highly uncertain future that summer. Dobson had hoped to use the Malton plant to build the Tudor, a civilian transport version of the Lancaster. Dobson tried to interest TCA in buying the aircraft but the national airline was non-committal. In July, Howe publicly announced his plan to sell Victory Aircraft to Hawker Siddeley and build civilian aircraft to sell to airlines such as TCA. Dobson also tried and failed to interest the RCAF in the Tudor, and the Hawker Siddeley board back in England was dubious about Dobson's Canadian scheme.

As summer turned to fall, Dobson kept working on his plan, while Smye waited nervously back in Canada. Dobson then returned to Ottawa, where on November 2, he and Howe reached a formal deal similar to their informal arrangement of June for Victory Aircraft. Dobson agreed to buy "the whole bloody thing" for $2.5 million, which wouldn't be payable until the firm generated profits. Howe got a promise that the new concern would be run by Canadians and would design and develop its own aircraft. When the deal took effect a month later, the new firm was called A.V. Roe Canada.

Although the new firm got immediate work converting Lancasters for RCAF postwar work, the idea of producing Tudors had already been dismissed. Dobson and Smye were instead talking about producing an all-new aircraft to carry passengers across Canada, which would be powered by a new type of engine that had first seen use in the war—the jet engine.

CHAPTER 3

The Jet

WORLD WAR II WAS A LENGTHY struggle in which the opposing militaries fought hard for advantage, using new technologies and new tactics. Aircraft and armoured vehicles such as tanks, as well as new technologies such as radar and code breaking played decisive roles. The war also saw the introduction of guided missiles by the Germans, and more importantly, the atomic bomb by the United States.

The field of aircraft technology was revolutionized during the war. In the 1930s, biplanes were still in wide use, and metal-skinned aircraft carrying passengers were just coming into common use. Aircraft companies, air racers and researchers were improving aircraft, making bigger loads and higher speeds possible. The war clouds that gathered over the world in the late 1930s gave impetus to aircraft makers, especially in Germany, Japan, Great Britain, the Soviet Union and the United States, to build aircraft for use in the coming conflict.

Once the war began, spending picked up as the combatants battled for any technological advantage they could win in the air. Some aircraft increased in size to carry more and bigger bombs, and others flew at higher speeds and gained agility for the great air battles of the war. Radar-guidance equipment and anti-aircraft weapons were also advanced technologically. In the U.S., the National Advisory Committee for Aeronautics (NACA), a U.S. government agency, conducted research on aerodynamics and engines for aircraft in laboratories in Virginia, Ohio and California. The results of NACA's work were shared with the growing U.S. aircraft industry, which developed innovations of its own.

The propeller engines that powered most of the aircraft involved in the war were made more powerful and more efficient. But throughout the war, another type of engine that used a new type of propulsion was tested and flown.

Although rockets powered by gunpowder had been around for centuries, the modern liquid-fuelled rocket was only created in the 1920s and '30s. This rocket carries fuel and oxidizer in separate tanks; when the liquids are mixed together, they produce thrust. As the war approached, engineers and scientists looked at using rocket engines for aircraft as well as a similar type of engine that became known as the jet engine. Jets carry their fuel like rockets but draw their oxidizer from the air and then mix the two substances to produce thrust. For aircraft, jets are lighter, more efficient and easier to operate than rockets.

The first country off the mark with jet aircraft was Germany. On August 27, 1939, just a few days before the war began with Adolf Hitler's invasion of Poland,

Erich Warsitz flew the first aircraft powered by a jet engine. The aircraft, designed by Ernst Heinkel, had jet engines designed by Hans von Ohain, a graduate of Göttingen University. Warsitz had earlier distinguished himself by flying the first rocket planes in association with Heinkel and German rocket pioneer Wernher von Braun. Now that the jet engine showed more promise, the Heinkel and Messerschmitt companies set to work on building jets. The only jet aircraft deployed in any significant numbers during the war was the Me 262 jet fighter, which entered combat in July 1944. Although, at 870 kilometres per hour, it flew faster than any other plane and scored against Allied bombers and fighters, the Allied air forces devised strategies to destroy the Me 262 on the ground and exploit its poor maneuverability in the air.

In 1941, a British aircraft flew with a jet engine designed by Frank Whittle, whose pioneering work in the 1930s had been slowed by the British government's lack of interest. Although both British and American aircraft firms began working with jet engines, Britain's Gloster Meteor was the only Allied jet aircraft used during the war. T.A. Heppenheimer explained in his history of flight that American and British aircraft with supercharged piston engines were already able to fly higher and faster than most other aircraft of the day, so deploying jet aircraft was not seen as a priority. The Germans, who did not have supercharged engines, tried with their Me 262 jet to leapfrog American aircraft with supercharged engines such as the P-38 Lightning and the P-51 Mustang. While both the Me 262

and the Meteor could fly faster than any propeller aircraft, the two jets proved to be of limited military use
because they were tricky to fly.

Midway during the war, C.D. Howe and his top
assistant for aircraft production, Ralph Bell, visited
England, where they were briefed on the work with
Whittle's turbojet engines, and the two Canadians
decided to look into the possibility of Canada taking
part in the development of these new engines. Up to
that time, Canada had no experience in aircraft
engines. All aircraft made in Canada before and during World War II were powered with engines made in
Great Britain or the United States.

A group of Canadian experts sent by Howe and Bell
visited England and reported on how Canada could
take part in jet engine development. As a result,
Howe's Munitions Ministry decided to set up a facility in Winnipeg to test jet engines, starting with
engines built in England, and they established a jet
compressor plant at a former explosives plant in
Nobel, Ontario, near Parry Sound. Researchers from
the ministry and the National Research Council of
Canada (NRC) began work on jet engines in 1943,
and soon they set up a facility in Toronto to coordi-
nate research and development of these engines. The
operation was set up as a Crown corporation called
Turbo Research. The new firm was still in the early
stages of its work when the war ended, and it was put
on the block with other war-related Crown corpora-
tions such as Victory Aircraft.

At war's end, both the American and British aircraft industries began to look to the future, of which jet engines formed a central part. Jet engines could be used for the next generation of fighter aircraft and for transport aircraft carrying passengers and cargo. Because the British were further ahead in jets, they continued to deploy the Gloster Meteor with the RAF and set to work on designing jet transports. The Americans also began looking at jet fighter aircraft. On their testing grounds (such as what would become Edwards Air Force Base in the California desert), they began trials on jet and rocket planes, which, by 1947, would be flying faster than the speed of sound. Amid all this activity, people such as Roy Dobson at Hawker Siddeley, Fred Smye at Avro Canada and C.D. Howe, whose Munitions and Supply Department was now known as the Department of Reconstruction and Supply, were preoccupied with deciding the future of Canada's aircraft industry in the postwar world.

CHAPTER 4

The Jetliner

EVEN BEFORE HE HAD WON CONTROL of the firm that became Avro Canada, Roy Dobson was already talking to C.D. Howe and officials at Trans-Canada Air Lines, Canada's national air carrier, about building jet transports. TCA had started operations in 1937, and after the war, the company was ready to expand operations and buy new aircraft. Just as the sale of Victory Aircraft was closing in November 1945, Dobson sent one of his top engineers from Manchester, Stuart "Dave" Davies, to Canada to join Fred Smye in meeting TCA management about a new type of aircraft.

TCA was enthusiastic about jet aircraft, especially after hearing about the new AJ65 Avon jet engine that Rolls-Royce in Britain was developing. TCA and Avro discussed the possibility of creating an aircraft that would be powered by two Avons, have a range of 1800 kilometres and carry 36 passengers at a speed of nearly 700 kilometres per hour.

Avro Canada also went to work on assembling a team of engineers to work on the new aircraft and the CF-100, a military jet program. As befits a firm with strong British ties, the Avro Canada's team at Malton attracted a group of Canadians with a large contingent of British engineers and tradespeople, starting at the top with people such as James C. Floyd and John Frost. Many of them came to Canada to escape the postwar austerity still gripping life in Britain, as well as an aircraft industry that suffered from stifling rules and customs and from postwar retrenchment of the defence industry. They hoped to find opportunity in Canada's growing aircraft industry. Canada was more attractive than the U.S. because, at the time, it still had strong links and similarities to the United Kingdom.

Floyd came from Avro in England in 1946 to head up design of the Jetliner, and Frost joined Avro in June 1947 to direct the effort on the CF-100. Among the top Canadians was Mario A. Pesando, a University of Toronto graduate who had started at Victory Aircraft when the Lancaster program was just beginning and stayed on at Malton with Avro. From Noorduyn Aircraft in Montreal, Carl V. Lindow and James A. Chamberlin were hired for the engineering staff.

Early in 1946, TCA gave Avro Canada a letter of intent in which it promised to buy Avro's new transport plane, which soon became known as the C-102 Jetliner. The letter contained strict conditions regarding the cost of the aircraft and delivery dates. Making or attempting to meet promises on either count is very dangerous for aircraft makers, especially when a technology is new, as was the case with the jet transports. Most aircraft companies were used to contracts with government agencies run on a cost-plus basis, in which costs are allowed to increase and the contractor

is guaranteed a profit. As with any other manufactured item, the cost of each Jetliner would depend in
part on how many were ordered, which meant that
a large number of Jetliners would need to be made to
meet TCA's price. The matter was complicated by
TCA's refusal to state how many aircraft it planned to
buy. By the end of 1946, Avro knew that it would
likely not be able to meet TCA's price, but the airline
refused to budge from the terms of its letter.

In the spring of 1947, Dobson was brought in to get
Howe's support for the Jetliner, and Howe's Department of Reconstruction and Supply agreed to help
finance the building of the first Jetliners. But at the
same time, Rolls-Royce announced that its Avon
engines wouldn't be ready for some time. So the aircraft's design was changed to incorporate four Rolls-
Royce Derwent engines, similar to the engines already
proven in the Gloster Meteor fighter. Use of the Der-
wents meant major design changes for the Jetliner,
and worse, these engines were not as efficient as the
Avons, which meant higher fuel costs for the plane,
making it less attractive for airlines. The result was
that TCA remained firm in its refusal to buy the Jetliner because the aircraft could not fly far enough or
efficiently enough to meet TCA's requirements.

But with backing from the Canadian government,
Floyd and his team at Avro pressed on with the Jetliner. Because it was in a race with the de Havilland
Comet in England, to be the world's first jet transport
aircraft, the Jetliner's design incorporated many new
features. Jim Chamberlin included a new concept

involving double flaps on the Jetliner's elevators and rudders to allow better control of the aircraft. The Jetliner was also designed for shorter haul flights than the Comet. While the British aircraft was aimed at the transatlantic market, which was just opening up, Avro hoped to sell the Jetliner for shorter routes in North America, which were already being served with propeller aircraft.

The Jetliner took to the air for the first time at Malton on August 10, 1949, and flew for an hour at altitudes up to 4000 metres. But the Jetliner would not have the title of the world's first jet transport, because the Comet had taken to the air for the first time two weeks earlier in England. So the Jetliner could only claim a North American "first." Despite the lack of any firm orders for the aircraft, Avro pressed on with flight testing, and in April 1950, the Jetliner became the first jet transport to fly in the United States when it journeyed to New York, where it received heavy and favourable press coverage. The *Rochester Democrat and Chronicle* said the Jetliner's performance "should give our nation a good kick in its placidity. The fact that our massive but underpopulated good neighbour to the north has a mechanical product that licks anything of ours is just what the doctor ordered for our overdeveloped ego."

But the Jetliner program was already flying in stormy weather, and more storms lay just ahead.

CHAPTER 5

The Cold War

ON THE EVENING OF Wednesday, September 5, 1945, just three days after Japan's formal surrender brought an end to World War II, a nervous 26-year-old clerk from the Soviet embassy in Ottawa walked into the newsroom of the *Ottawa Journal* and tried to persuade the night city editor that the documents he carried on him portended war with the Soviet Union. Igor Gouzenko was nearing the end of his two-year tour of duty in Canada encoding cable traffic between his embassy and Moscow, and he had decided that he did not want to go home. His poor command of English and his nervous manner put off the editor. Later that same evening, a commissionaire turned Gouzenko away from the closed Department of Justice building. The next day, Royal Canadian Mounted Police (RCMP) officers followed Gouzenko and his wife, Svetlana, as the couple tried and failed to gain political asylum in government offices and then, afraid that Soviet agents would try to grab them, sought refuge in a neighbour's apartment.

Late that evening, officers from the Soviet embassy arrived at the Gouzenko apartment and ransacked it in search of the documents Gouzenko had taken.

The Ottawa Police arrived and allowed the Soviet officers to leave when they claimed diplomatic immunity,
and the RCMP picked up the Gouzenkos. They were
given asylum and taken to a secret location where the
Mounties and other government officials began to go
through Gouzenko's story and the documents he had
taken with him from the embassy.

Gouzenko's defection to Canada was kept secret
until the following February 15, when Mackenzie
King made a vague announcement that unspecified
persons had passed information to an unnamed foreign embassy. But the same morning, the RCMP had
raided the homes of Canadian civil servants and others implicated by Gouzenko, and word of the arrests
and Gouzenko's defection soon filtered out. Rumours
suggested that the Soviets had operated a gigantic spy
ring seeking information related to the atomic bomb
and other military secrets.

The news of the Gouzenko affair and the subsequent Royal Commission and trial of those caught as
a result of Gouzenko's revelations, which included a
Member of Parliament, jarred Canadians and others
who had become used to seeing the Soviet Union as a
friendly ally in the war against Nazi Germany. During
the war, the Soviets had been depicted in a positive
light in Western media, and the sacrifices made by
Soviet troops at Stalingrad and in other epic battles
deeply impressed Canadians, Americans and Europe-
ans. Many people hoped that the alliance would out-
live World War II, if only to provide a respite to the
hardships that war brought, even to those separated

from the battle zones by the Atlantic and Pacific Oceans. But those hopes began to fade in the fall of 1945 as Soviet officials registered strong disagreements with American, British and French officials in talks over postwar Europe.

In early 1946, prompted in part by Gouzenko's revelations, U.S. President Harry Truman and other Americans began to take a more critical attitude to the Soviet Union. On March 5, former British Prime Minister Winston Churchill visited Fulton, Missouri, at Truman's invitation and gave a speech warning that an "iron curtain" had descended across the centre of Europe. Soviet takeovers of countries they occupied at war's end, including Poland, Bulgaria, Romania, Hungary, Czechoslovakia, Yugoslavia and Albania, turned the rift into a conflict that soon became known as the Cold War. The Soviets also controlled parts of Germany and Austria, and Truman took action against communist partisans in Greece and strong communist parties in France and Italy.

As a result of the growing tensions between the U.S. and its allies on one side, and the Soviets and its satellite states on the other, Western governments realized that they would have to be well armed to protect their populations against possible Soviet aggression. In 1949, Western European nations joined with Canada and the United States in the North Atlantic Treaty Organization (NATO), which formalized the presence of American and Canadian forces in Europe to protect against a Soviet invasion. That fall, Mao Zedong's communist forces finally won their long civil war and took control of the world's most populous country, China, increasing the communist threat.

Another element in the Cold War was nuclear weapons. The United States dropped the first atomic bombs on Hiroshima and Nagasaki in August 1945, shortly before Japan surrendered. Truman announced that these new weapons had been the result of a massive, top-secret research effort that involved U.S. scientists who had help from colleagues in Great Britain and Canada. Despite the secrecy that surrounded the bombs, spies in the ranks of the scientists had informed Soviet authorities of their work, and Soviet dictator Josef Stalin launched a crash effort to build a Soviet atomic bomb. That effort bore fruit on August 29, 1949, when the first Soviet atomic bomb was successfully detonated. The test was secret, but American intelligence officials soon learned of it from fallout that drifted outside the Soviet boundaries, and Truman's announcement that the Soviets possessed the bomb marked a dangerous new phase in the conflict between East and West.

Although the news of the Soviet bomb surprised many members of the public, Western government officials knew from the moment of the creation of the first atomic bomb that the Soviets would work hard to develop nuclear weapons. The creation of Soviet nuclear weapons meant that Soviet aircraft could conceivably attack the United States with their deadly cargo. But first they would have to pass over or near Canadian territory.

CHAPTER 6

The CF-100

IN THE MONTHS FOLLOWING the end of the war, the small workforce at Avro Canada in Malton began designing a jet interceptor aircraft for the RCAF that became known as the CF-100. The Canadian government had decided at war's end that the RCAF should be able to defend Canadian airspace with its own aircraft. The RCAF looked at aircraft being developed in the U.S. and Great Britain but decided that none filled Canada's requirements. That led the RCAF to look to the Canadian industry, specifically Avro Canada, to develop an all-new aircraft. The RCAF asked for a two-seater that had two jet engines and would fly at 900 kilometres per hour (Mach .85) at an altitude of 12,000 metres with a range of 1200 kilometres. They sought an interceptor that would be capable of operating at any time of day in a full range of weather conditions.

To build a jet engine for the RCAF's new interceptor, Avro quickly picked up Turbo Research Ltd., the firm set up by the Canadian government to work on jet engines, and Turbo became the Gas Turbine Division of Avro Canada. The division first built a research engine known as the Chinook, and then began to work on the Orenda engines that would power the

The CF-100

~◦✕◦~

CF-100. At first, development of the CF-100 and its engine went slowly, but as the dimensions of the Cold War became clearer following the Gouzenko affair, Canadian government interest in the CF-100 grew. The CF-100 program took a major risk in that it married an untried aircraft design with an untried engine, the Orenda, contrary to many previous aircraft, which usually involved new airframes and proven engines.

The explosion of the first Soviet A-bomb in 1949 demonstrated that the United States and its allies, including Canada, had to face up to the possibility of Soviet nuclear attack. By then, the Soviet Union had shown that it was serious about building heavy bombers that could deliver atomic bombs. As the war was ending, Stalin had ordered his aircraft designers to reverse engineer the American B-29 Superfortress, and this became possible when three of the American bombers made a forced landing in the Soviet Union. The result of this effort was the Tupolev Tu-4, and more advanced bombers followed as the Cold War continued.

The CF-100, for its part, was destined to form an important part of Canada's defences in the early years of the Cold War against Soviet bombers flying over the North Pole and Canadian air space, carrying atomic bombs on their way to targets in the United States and perhaps even southern Canada. Jim Chamberlin, who was still cutting his teeth on aircraft design at a time when jet aircraft were new and most existing performance data had been captured from the Germans, had headed up design on the CF-100 until John Frost came on board in 1947, 18 months into the program. Frost came with experience from de Havilland in England, and he pressed on with the new aircraft despite strong differences with Chamberlin that persisted throughout the program.

The Avro team completed the first CF-100 in 1949, and to fly the prototype, Avro brought in British test pilot Bill Waterton. He flew the aircraft, equipped with Rolls-Royce Avon engines, for the first time on January 19, 1950. The first flight was successful, but on the third flight, Waterton found a serious defect in the aircraft: because of changes in the placement of the two jet engines, the structural supports for the engines could not withstand the loads and the flexing of the main wing spar. Other problems also cropped up, such as the aircraft's weight and fuel lines, as well as canopy ejection issues and a difficulty with ejecting the rear seat. As well, there were troubles with the armament for the aircraft, and later with its extended wings. In April 1951, a CF-100 crashed and claimed the life of its pilot, Flight Lieutenant Bruce Warren, and observer Robert Ostrander.

As the Avro engineers grappled with the CF-100's problems and tried to find a market for the company's new Jetliner, events on the other side of the Earth brought big changes for Avro as the Cold War moved into a new and dangerous phase.

~∞C~

CHAPTER 7

Korea

IN THE EARLY HOURS of June 25, 1950, thousands of troops in the North Korean army, equipped with tanks and aircraft from the Soviet Union, crossed the border and invaded South Korea. The Korean penninsula had been occupied for most of the century by Japan, but when the Japanese surrendered to end World War II, American forces occupied the southern part of the country to the 38th parallel, and Soviet forces occupied northern Korea. The occupation had been agreed to by the two powers, and as their wartime alliance gave way to Cold War confrontation, the two sides dug in and established friendly governments in their sectors of Korea, as they were also doing in occupied Europe. The Soviets and the North Korean government, led by Kim Il-Sung, believed that they could take over South Korea from the Americans without a fight, but their theory was proven wrong after their invasion of the south met resistance.

Led by the United States and under the United Nations flag (UN), a number of countries joined the Korean War. During the 13 months that would follow the North Korean invasion, most of the land area of Korea changed hands between the two sides in the first major armed confrontation of the Cold War. When United Nations forces conquered much of the north and came close to the border with China, Communist Chinese forces joined the North Koreans. Peace talks began in 1951 as sporadic fighting continued, and an armistice was reached two years later. For more than a half century since, the border between North and South Korea has remained a centre of military and diplomatic tension.

Canada took an active role in the UN force, sending nearly 27,000 soldiers into the fight, of whom 516 died. Korea marked Canada's last ground-combat war until it joined the fight in Afghanistan in 2002. The Korean War marked a new high point in Cold War tensions, and the Canadian government became more concerned about Canadian defences, including the troubled CF-100 interceptor.

The third CF-100, the first fitted with Orenda engines, made its maiden flight in June 1951. Although the Orenda engines worked well and would eventually be counted as the greatest strength of the CF-100, the other problems remained. C.D. Howe, by then Minister of Trade and Commerce and Minister of Defence Production, was angry that the aircraft was still suffering from problems at a time when it was so urgently needed. Controversy over the CF-100 delays spilled into the media and the House of Commons in Ottawa. Howe's concern, along with the political and media criticism of Avro, led him to order Avro to halt work on the Jetliner and concentrate on the CF-100. In early 1951, Avro reluctantly bowed to Howe's demands.

Howe's worries about Avro and the CF-100 were not entirely quieted with the company's efforts to fix the CF-100 and halt Jetliner production work. The result was a major shake-up at the aircraft firm in 1951. A.V. Roe Canada's first president, Walter Deisher, was replaced by Crawford Gordon. Gordon gave Deisher's number two, Fred Smye, full authority over Avro's aircraft programs.

Among the many changes Gordon and Smye made at Avro was moving Jim Floyd to the CF-100 project. To help fix the troublesome spar and other problems dogging the aircraft, Floyd brought in Robert N. Lindley, who he had worked with in England. Lindley, a blunt, no-nonsense manager, took Waclaw Czerwinski out of the Jetliner stress office and put him on the team he had formed to deal with the CF-100 spar problem, and Czerwinski soon developed an effective fix. John Frost was moved to special projects, and Gordon created separate divisions for engines and aircraft. The CF-100 entered regular production and full service in the RCAF just as the Korean War ended in 1953.

Meanwhile, Avro continued to keep alive its hope of selling the Jetliner to customers in the United States. One such effort involved flying the Jetliner to California, where for several months, it became the personal plaything of eccentric millionaire Howard Hughes, who owned, among other things, Trans-World Airlines (TWA). Several Avro employees flew to the Hughes airfield in the Los Angeles suburb of Culver City to run some flight tests on the Jetliner, but their stay stretched into weeks as Hughes asked to continue to fly the Jetliner.

Hughes' interest in the Jetliner became one of the more colourful sidelights of the Avro Canada story. The Avro engineers who went to California with the Jetliner came to know the millionaire, who was not yet the recluse that he later notoriously became. Hughes put up his Canadian guests in a luxury Hollywood hotel suite, but the Canadians soon learned that Hughes never carried money on him and was always asking for change for phone calls or to gas up his car.

Along with other airlines in the U.S., TWA considered ordering Jetliners, but the orders were stopped cold by Howe's insistence that the CF-100 program command all of Avro's resources. The Jetliner needed more development work before it would be ready for use by airlines, and Howe did not want to spend government resources on the aircraft while the CF-100 was urgently needed. Also, Avro could not induce airlines to help pay the development costs. So by the time the CF-100 program was on track, the Jetliner's moment had passed.

One of Canada's top aviation experts, Larry Milberry, had a harsh assessment of the Jetliner. He said the aircraft's fuselage and wings were not particularly efficient for the speeds at which the jet engines could move it. The plane's switch to four Derwent engines further reduced its efficiency and made it unsuitable for TCA's use because it could not fly far enough. American airlines would not likely have bought the

aircraft even had the Jetliner not been blocked by
Howe because they would have been reluctant to buy
an aircraft equipped with foreign engines, and the
Buy America Act would have impeded sales as well.
Even Boeing, which was moving ahead in the 1950s
with its own jet transports, had to overcome resistance
from airlines reluctant to switch from aircraft with
propellers to jet engines. Milberry also noted that
there was no interest in the Jetliner in the United
Kingdom or elsewhere in Europe. The type of market
that would have been served by the Jetliner, inter-
urban routes that did not involve crossing continents
or oceans, did not open to smaller jets until 1991 with
the Canadair Regional Jet. In his *Air Transport in Canada*, Milberry wrote, "the Jetliner was a bold new concept, but an inordinately costly one, ill-timed and
ill-executed."

Avro's James Floyd has hit back at questions that
were raised about the saleability of the Jetliner, outlining the interest shown by TWA and National Airlines in versions of the Jetliner powered by Rolls-Royce
Nene engines or Pratt and Whitney J-57 engines,
which would offer greater efficiency and range.

The sole Jetliner continued to be flown by Avro to
support the CF-100 program as a test platform or
to carry photographers. But after its last flight in
November 1956, the Jetliner was dismantled. To
those at Avro who worked on the aircraft, its loss
was heartbreaking. They didn't know that even more
heartbreak was on the way.

CHAPTER 8

The Canuck

AVRO'S FLIGHT TEST DEPARTMENT had its work cut out for it tracking down the problems and testing the fixes on the CF-100. Pilots were busy testing the aircraft for its various roles and preparing it for use with its different weapons systems. Avro employees Fred Matthews and Peter J. Armitage were both slated to fly in the backseat of the CF-100 as part of the flight-test program. Both cheated death when they missed flights for medical reasons and the observers who took their places died in crashes.

Matthews was convinced that the observer who died in his place had been doomed by a canopy that did not come off when it should have. Matthews started looking through results of wind tunnel tests on the CF-100, and he found that the canopy covering the plane's backseat was not the same shape as the model used in the wind tunnel. He ordered a flight test using a spare canopy drilled with holes for pressure gauges. When that test flight was inconclusive, he installed more pressure gauges and, on the next flight, proved his theory that the canopy was not the right shape to come off during an ejection. "All aeroplanes were grounded and the canopies were redesigned," said Matthews.

But the redesigned canopies didn't solve what would prove to be the greatest danger for the observers who flew in the backseat of the CF-100. After missing a flight in which the pilot ejected safely but the observer died still strapped in his seat, Armitage realized that the observer couldn't reach up and pull the overhead ejection handle because of the slipstream that formed if the aircraft was flying above a certain speed. The solution turned out to be simple: install a windshield in front of the observer.

To make sure the fixes worked, Avro organized a series of tests of the ejection system from the rear seat of the CF-100, some with George, the Avro test dummy. With Avro test pilot Jan Zurakowski at the controls, former RAF Squadron Leader Pat Fifield, then a test pilot with the ejection seat manufacturer Martin-Baker, ejected safely from the backseat of the CF-100.

The CF-100's official top speed was Mach 0.85, but Zurakowski and other test pilots managed to fly it at supersonic speeds, which could be done safely in a dive under specific conditions. Many in the engineering department didn't believe that the aircraft had broken the sound barrier, so Mario Pesando and Zurakowski conspired to have a CF-100 break the sound barrier during a meeting held to discuss this controversy. According to Pesando, the double sonic boom from the CF-100 quickly brought the meeting to an end.

The CF-100 was officially known as the "Canuck." Those who flew it called it the "Clunk," the "Lead Sled," "CF-Zero," the "Zilch" and many other names. Although the seats were uncomfortable, the cockpit layout difficult and the heating inadequate, the CF-100 effectively did the job it was designed to do, and when necessary, more, as Zurakowski demonstrated with his supersonic dive and other acrobatic feats with the aircraft. The CF-100 successfully carried out its mission of patrolling Canadian skies in the early years of the Cold War.

By late 1958, when the last CF-100 rolled off the assembly line at Malton, Avro had built 692 CF-100s. The RCAF deployed the aircraft in nine squadrons around Canada and four in Europe before replacing it in 1963. A few CF-100s remained in service for research and for electronic warfare training until the Canadian Forces retired the aircraft in 1981. The CF-100 had been a success, and it remains the only all-Canadian jet interceptor put into active service. The many problems that plagued the CF-100 during its development turned C.D. Howe and other politicians into harsh critics of Avro, but they also taught the Avro engineers and designers some valuable lessons.

Avro made many efforts to sell the CF-100 to other air forces but only succeeded in selling 53 to the Belgian Air Force. All efforts to sell the aircraft to the United States Air Force (USAF) failed. As Lester B. Pearson, a prominent member of the Liberal government of the 1950s and a future prime minister, told the House of Commons: "The aircraft industry down there was not going to allow any interference with its own right to produce its own aircraft for its own government."

The CF-100's engine, the Orenda, did much better in the marketplace than the CF-100, with nearly 4000 built at the Orenda engine plant in Malton. The engines were also built to power the North American F-86 Sabre fighters constructed under licence by Canadair in Montreal for use by the RCAF in Korea and Europe. Some of the Canadian-built Sabres were also sold to West Germany, South Africa and Colombia.

The CF-100 had been a big gamble for Avro because it married an untried aircraft with a brand new engine. The success of this gamble would encourage Avro's new management to gamble again. The RCAF's orders for the CF-100 and the Orenda engine kept Avro's large workforce busy, and with the prospect of a new aircraft to replace the CF-100 giving Avro Canada an apparently bright future, Avro Canada became much more than just a builder of aircraft. The fact that the Jetliner never sold and the CF-100, for all its success, saw limited sales in the aircraft marketplace did not darken the dreams of the new management at Avro Canada.

CHAPTER 9

Crawford Gordon

IN OCTOBER 1951, just as Avro's crisis over the CF-100 was at its height, Walter Deisher stepped down as president of A.V. Roe Canada Ltd. and was replaced by a dynamic 36-year-old associate of C.D. Howe, named Crawford Gordon II. While the delays with the CF-100 lay at the heart of Howe's dissatisfaction with Avro, Howe also had misgivings about Deisher and the management at Avro.

By 1951, Gordon had spent the better part of his working career under Howe's tutelage, first at the Department of Munitions and Supply as director general of organization and assistant coordinator of defence production. Gordon remained with Howe after the war, helping companies reconvert from wartime to peacetime work, and in 1947, Gordon returned to the electrical appliance business, where he had worked before the war. When the Korean War began, Howe set up the Department of Defence Production (DDP) and appointed Gordon as the director of production, where he worked for several months until he got the top job at Avro Canada and the assignment to bring order to the troubled firm.

At the time, *Saturday Night* magazine described Gordon as a "hard-hitting, blunt businessman." His biographer, Greig Stewart, wrote: "Anyone who ever had anything to do with Crawford Gordon, men and women alike, never forgot him. They either hated him or loved him." When he took over Avro, Gordon was already losing his hair and gaining heft on his frame, but his charm, which one observer claimed "just about dropped the pants off every lady he met" remained undiminished.

Gordon was born on December 26, 1914, in Winnipeg, the son of an executive with the Canadian Imperial Bank of Commerce. His mother had survived the sinking of the *Titanic* in 1912. Gordon's childhood included six years in Jamaica, a sojourn in England, and finally a stay in Toronto, following his father's work transfers with the bank. Gordon attended McGill University, where he earned a B.Sc. in 1936. That year he met his future wife, Mary Tierney, whom he married in 1937. They had a son and two daughters. Gordon worked for Canadian General Electric but sought out a posting under Howe when the war broke out.

Avro Canada's new president was already familiar with the company's problems from his work at the Department of Defence Production, and he moved quickly to reorganize Avro. First, Gordon ordered a halt to all work on the second Jetliner and closed down a sales office that marketed the aircraft in the U.S., though lower-key sales efforts continued for a time. He then divided the company into aircraft and engine divisions. Although other managers were let

The stock offering turned Avro Canada from a British-controlled company into one in which Canadians held a substantial stake. According to James Dow's history of Avro, by 1958, Gordon presided over a colossus that controlled nearly 40 companies with a total of 41,000 employees, assets of $300 million and net annual sales of $380 million in the uninflated money of the time. Besides aircraft, Avro Canada was moving into coal and steel production, electronics, rolling stock and shipbuilding. That year, Avro Canada was the third-largest corporation in Canada, behind Canadian Pacific and Alcan.

Avro became known for its aggressive and extensive public relations efforts, which included an Avro Choir and the Avro-Orenda Pipe Band, both of which performed free at charity and community functions in the Toronto area. Avro's security force was larger than many small-town police forces, and employee services at Avro built homes for some employees and maintained housing listings for others. Negotiations between Avro and its unionized work force were major efforts. More than 5000 cars used the company parking lot in Malton each day, and the traffic jams at shift changes were said to be the worst in Canada at the time. Avro executives entertained guests and held meetings in a mansion known as Briarcrest, which was not far from the plant and had served as the home of Walter Deisher until he sold it to the company.

Despite the company's diversification, Avro's main business was still building military aircraft. When the chief of the Air Staff, Air Marshall Wilf Curtis, retired from the RCAF in 1953, he was quickly offered a seat on the board of Avro Canada, which he accepted. When the CF-100 assembly line wound down in 1958, Avro planned to have another, more advanced aircraft to replace it. This aircraft got its start in the anxious days of the early 1950s.

CHAPTER 10

The Arrow's First Controversy

EVEN BEFORE THE FIRST CF-100 rolled off the assembly line in 1949, the RCAF and Avro were thinking about the plane's successor. The probability of better and faster Soviet bombers and fighters passing through Canadian airspace, along with the birth of the supersonic era in 1947, meant that the CF-100 would quickly become obsolete. The Canadian and American governments also began talking about building radar defences that began with a string of stations along the 50th parallel, known as the Pinetree Line. Later on, two more strings of radar stations were built, the Mid-Canada Line that involved radar stations built along the 55th parallel, and finally the Distant Early Warning (DEW) Line, built along the 70th parallel in Canada's Arctic and Alaska.

The RCAF wanted an aircraft that, when alerted by radars, could quickly be scrambled to block the routes Soviet bombers might take to targets in southern Canada and the United States. The RCAF assembled a small team in 1948 to begin drawing up specifications for the successor to the CF-100, and the group suggested a tailless, delta-winged aircraft. Although this represented a departure from the straight-winged

CF-100, the new aircraft would have two engines and a crew of two, a pilot and a navigator, as did the CF-100. People at Avro were also looking ahead in 1948, and a group that included Edgar Atkin, then the chief engineer, and Jim Chamberlin, began to think about how the CF-100 design could be adapted for the future. They came up with three ideas, including what constituted a CF-100 with swept wings. The ideas passed between Avro and the RCAF, and in March 1952, the RCAF completed what became known as the "Final Report of the All-Weather Interceptor Requirements Team." Avro replied with two proposals, one known as the C-104/1, which had one engine, and the C-104/2, which had two engines. Both carried one pilot. The proposals also spoke of various possible jet engines, including a Curtiss Wright J67 engine, a Rolls Royce RB-106 jet engine, a Bristol Olympus engine, or an engine being developed at Avro called the TR-9. The proposed aircraft would be equipped with Falcon missiles that were being designed by Hughes Aircraft in the U.S., and they could use a Hughes navigation and guidance system to help the pilot.

While these discussions were going on, the RCAF issued a document entitled Operational Requirement 1/1-63, "Supersonic All-Weather Interceptor Aircraft." When such a requirement was issued, the RCAF was obliged to find out if an aircraft that met the specifications in the document could be found on the open market. This meant sending an evaluation team to the U.S., England and France, where aircraft contractors were developing several fighter and interceptor aircraft. The team did not find a suitable aircraft, so the RCAF consulted the Department of Defence Production about procuring the aircraft in Canada, which meant from Avro Canada.

C.D. Howe headed up the DDP, and even though his protégé Crawford Gordon was in charge at Malton, Howe was not pleased to hear about the possibility of Avro building a new aircraft. "The minister had been making himself somewhat of a gadfly for Avro with his constant badgering for production of the CF-100," James Dow wrote in his history of the Arrow. "Now the news of another project left him in a sour mood."

A few days before Christmas, Howe wrote the Minister of National Defence, Brooke Claxton. "Before authorizing [the new aircraft], I think you should appreciate what has already been spent on the Orenda engine and on the CF-100 to date," he wrote. "I must say I am frightened for the first time in my defence production experience...I must tell you that the design staff at Avro is far from competent to undertake work of this importance. Their designing record to date is very bad indeed, measured by any standard." Howe went on to suggest that further design work for the new aircraft should be contracted out to an established British firm.

Claxton, who was known to have more confidence in the Avro team, declined to take his colleague's advice. He took the proposed interceptor to the Cabinet Defence Committee and, in April 1953, came out with its agreement to have Avro begin work on a mock-up of the aircraft as well as a prototype, and to begin testing equipment. The initial outlay was a modest $200,000 in a contract that covered costs, plus a five percent fee. The RCAF issued Specification AIR 7-3 for "Design Studies of Prototype Supersonic All-Weather Interceptor Aircraft," which called for a two-engined aircraft with a combat radius of action of 370 kilometres at supersonic speeds and 550 kilometres at subsonic speeds.

The specifications in this document were used to design what became the CF-105 Avro Arrow, and years later, these specifications became one of many controversies that surrounded the aircraft.

The man who headed up the technical effort on the Arrow, James Floyd, summed up his feelings this way in an interview with Greig Stewart: "What the air staff were asking for was the moon. In short, they required a two-place, twin-engined aircraft with all-weather reliability, long-range short takeoff and landing, an internal weapons compartment as large as the bomb bay of a B-29, and a supersonic maneuverability of 2 G at Mach 1.5 at 15,000 metres, without any loss of speed or altitude—a requirement which has been met by few, if any, service aircraft even to this day [the 1980s]. In addition, it was to be guided by the most sophisticated automatic flight and fire-control system ever envisaged."

Two assumptions underlying the early decisions on the new aircraft have come into question. One was that the Arrow would fully replace the CF-100, which was used by regular RCAF squadrons and reserve squadrons, requiring more than 600 aircraft. The RCAF specifications, by their very nature, brought into question whether the new aircraft would be as easy to operate as the CF-100 and therefore be open to use by reserve pilots.

And then there was the question of the RCAF's whole strategy. Instead of working jointly with the U.S. Air Force on our northern defence, the RCAF chose to go on its own and procure its own aircraft, which meant building the new aircraft and its infrastructure.

But in 1953, the problems of the CF-105 were still in the future. Avro was overcoming issues with the CF-100s and was gearing up production. By December of that year, the Cabinet Defence Committee had agreed to spend nearly $27 million on a five-year development program for the new interceptor that included the construction of two prototypes, which was the traditional pattern for these types of development programs. The beginning of this new aircraft program appeared to guarantee Avro's future, despite the doubts of C.D. Howe and others.

～✖～

CHAPTER 11

Early Days

IN 1954, SOON AFTER the CF-105 program began in earnest, the Soviet Union unveiled its new bomber, the jet-powered Myasishchev M-4 "Bison," and before long the Soviets began flying their most successful bomber of the Cold War, the turboprop Tupolev Tu-95 "Bear." Combined with the successful explosion of the first Soviet hydrogen bomb in 1953, the arrival of these bombers added urgency to Canada's need for a supersonic interceptor.

The Canadian government and the RCAF, together with the United States, were charged with defending Canada and much of the United States against these bombers, and the two governments were already working together on radars such as the DEW Line, the Pinetree Line and the Mid-Canada Line. The Americans were also working on their own bombers (the most successful of which was the Boeing B-52 Stratofortress, which remains in service to this day, more than 50 years after it was first deployed), and an array of interceptors, missiles, sophisticated computer systems and other weapons to defend against Soviet bombers.

As Canada and the United States built up their defences in 1954, Avro proposed a new development and testing program for the CF-105 that would cost $118 million and lead to the production of 40 aircraft, which Avro saw as the start of a much larger production run. More importantly, this plan abandoned the traditional procedure of building and testing one or two prototypes before the tooling for mass production was fabricated.

Avro's new plan reflected changes sweeping America's military aircraft business. Two USAF Major Generals, Deputy Chief of Staff for Materiel Orval R. Cook and Deputy Chief of Staff for Development Laurence C. Craigie, had proposed that the prototype step in the development cycle be eliminated and that production jigs be built at the beginning of an aircraft program so that the aircraft could move directly from the drawing board to the pre-production stage. This allowed for faster development and production cycles. Although this method, which became known as the Cook-Craigie plan, involved increased financial risk, it has since become standard for new aircraft projects, especially now that computer-assisted design allows aircraft to perform closer to predictions than before.

By this time, Rolls Royce had cancelled their RB-106 engine, which at the time had been Avro's first choice for the CF-105. Avro then began designing the aircraft to use the Curtiss-Wright J-67. Avro also decided to think about what it could do in-house at its Orenda Engines division. Research at Orenda Engines had concentrated on the TR-9 engine as the successor to the Orenda, but work on that engine was being set aside in the face of growing advances by other engine firms. Orenda instead proposed a new "two-spool" jet engine, which it saw moving ahead of the competition, but which would require a great deal of development work because its design involved a number of technical advances. According to Dow, design work on this new engine began in September 1953, with Avro supplying the money for the development program. When a test article of the PS-13 engine was first run on December 19, 1954, it worked in spite of vibration problems. By the time the Canadian government finally agreed to Avro's entreaties for financial help with the engine the following summer, Avro had already spent more than $8.5 million, most of which was picked up by the government.

The Canadian government finally approved Avro's CF-105 production proposal in March 1955, with the first four aircraft due for delivery in 1957. Avro and the RCAF reached agreements on a testing and development program for the aircraft, and prospects for Avro and the CF-105 looked bright that spring. But the engine issue arose again when the USAF abandoned the J-67 engine. The Canadian government soon agreed to equip the first five CF-105s with Pratt and Whitney J-75 engines, and then use Orenda's PS-13 engine, which was named the Iroquois. Suddenly the CF-105 program had become much more ambitious and potentially more expensive, because it now involved the development of a new airframe and a new engine.

The summer brought the first noticeable clouds to Avro's horizon. In June, Avro revised its cost estimates for the first 40 airframes to $153 million, and Fred Smye blamed the growing costs on "an increase in the scope of the work and the fact that the magnitude of the engineering effort required was not fully realized at the outset." Although Howe had shifted from his usual criticism of Avro in 1954 to praise the company's "efficient organization," that June he told the House of Commons: "We have embarked on a program of development which gives me the shudders, a supersonic plane and a supersonic engine."

By then, Brooke Claxton had left the defence portfolio and had been replaced by Ralph Campney, who decided to slow down the program, which pushed back the first deployment of CF-105s from 1960 to 1961. Campney was confronted with new cost estimates for the development of the aircraft, and the first 40 CF-105s of $298 million, well over twice the cost estimate Avro had provided in 1954. The RCAF also acknowledged that reserve squadrons could not fly the sophisticated Arrow, which meant that the RCAF would need only 300 CF-105s, not 600 or 700.

Two more major components of the CF-105 were facing major changes. First, the RCAF decided not to use the Hughes Falcon missile, mainly because the weapon was found to be unsuitable in a number of ways for use by the CF-105. Other plans to use the Canadian-designed Velvet Glove missile came to an end when the Velvet Glove was cancelled in 1955.

Instead, the RCAF opted for the Douglas Sparrow II air-to-air missile, which was still in development.

Avro still hoped to use the proven Hughes MX-1179 electronics system to run the aircraft's navigation, communications, interception and weapon fire control systems. However, according to Dow, Hughes refused to furnish the MX-1179 system by itself, but only in a package deal with the Falcon missile. So Avro was forced to turn to the Radio Corporation of America (RCA) to develop a brand-new fire-control system for the CF-105 in cooperation with Honeywell Controls and Computing Devices of Canada. This meant supporting RCA while it developed a brand-new fire system, the Astra I, and redesigning the CF-105 to take this new system. Although much of the work on Astra I would be done in Canada, the CF-105 program had once again become much more complicated and expensive. From a program that started with a new airframe and a proven engine, weapon and weapons fire-control system, the CF-105 now involved new and unproven versions of all four.

With Campney slowing down the program to spread out the CF-105's ballooning costs, the first murmurs of cancellation were heard in Ottawa. Fred Smye would later identify the change of weapons system, which brought with it the change of fire control system, as the "major cause of the cancellation" of the CF-105. Other issues also confronted the politicians in Ottawa as they considered the future of the CF-105, including the saleability of the aircraft in foreign markets.

CHAPTER 12

Growing Pains

THE GROWING COSTS of the CF-105 program and the fact that the RCAF would need only 300 aircraft meant that the economics of the program were changing for the worst. To keep costs down, Avro and the Canadian government needed to find foreign markets for the aircraft.

In early 1956, a British team from the RAF and the Royal Aeronautical Establishment (RAE) visited Malton to look over the CF-105. The British Minister of Supply, Reginald Maudling, later wrote Howe: "[I]n the rather changing circumstance, and particularly in the present financial stringency, the conclusion we finally reached was the CF-105 is not really suitable for our purposes." The conclusion could not have been a surprise to anyone; the British aircraft industry was in trouble because of tightening defence budgets, a fact that Avro Canada benefited from in the form of many highly trained engineers and other workers who came to Malton from British aircraft firms.

Around the same time, Ralph Campney made the first attempt to interest the U.S. military in the Arrow, but his sales pitch, as with the CF-100, was politely declined. As James Dow wrote: "Efforts to sell interceptors to the

Americans were blocked by the very logic that led Canada to build its own aircraft in the first place. Dependence on foreign sources for vital weapons systems was a potential threat to national security in an emergency. The U.S. government might have overlooked this threat in a source as close as Canada, but there was a very jealous American aircraft industry to contend with besides. Exporting jobs in this area would not be an astute political move." Dow also noted that three American aircraft contractors were competing for work to build what was called the Long-Range Interceptor, Experimental, or the F-108. Although the aircraft was never built, its planned existence proved another problem for Arrow sales to the United States.

During this time, the CF-105 program gained momentum, with testing of the airframe and its aero-dynamic shape, test runs of the Iroquois engine, and development of the Astra I electronics and fire-control system. In all these areas, Avro was moving to the leading edge of technology, something that represented opportunity but also danger. "The delicate balancing of separate but interdependent projects was, in some respects, a technological house of cards," Dow wrote. "The house would tremble when someone snapped out the card that read Sparrow II. Late in 1956, the United States Navy suddenly abandoned development of the Sparrow II air-to-air missile."

Avro and the RCAF could have chosen another missile, which would have meant changing the airframe and the Astra electronics system, or they could have paid the U.S. contractor Douglas to continue with the Sparrow II. Instead, they chose to move the Sparrow to Canada and continue development with an industry team headed by Avro. Canadair was chosen to work on the missile's airframe, and Canadian Westinghouse was selected to work on the missile's radar guidance system.

As 1957 dawned, Avro and the RCAF announced that the CF-105 would have a name: the Arrow. The name was a natural, given the plane's arrow-like shape. But the newly named Arrow was again facing political storms. The Liberal government reacted to the growing cost and complexity of the program by reducing the preproduction order of aircraft from 11 to 8, and continuing to plan for a next lot of 29 aircraft, which reduced the original order to 37 aircraft.

By then, C.D. Howe had gone to the Cabinet Defence Committee with a recommendation that the Arrow program be cancelled. But 1957 was an election year, and the Cabinet had no appetite to make such a decision until the election was over. The government had spent 22 uninterrupted years in power, and few people expected the Liberal Party's run of electoral good fortune would be broken that year. That feeling extended to the people toiling away on the CF-105.

CHAPTER 13

At the Leading Edge

As THE AVRO CANADA PLANT in Malton vibrated from the work generated by the fabrication of CF-100s in 1956 and 1957, it was also shaking from the noise generated by the testing of the new Iroquois engines. The first parts were being generated for the new aircraft, and jigs were being prepared for the production line that would begin with the first CF-105.

Avro's engineers and drafters produced more than 17,000 engineering drawings of the aircraft, and the 38,000 parts for each CF-105 came from 650 suppliers. The team, headed by Vice-President for Engineering Jim Floyd, Chief Engineer Robert Lindley and Chief of Technical Design Jim Chamberlin, included more than 2000 engineers. But the Arrow required more than drawings, parts, subcontractors, engineers, aerodynamicists, designers and drafters. With the Arrow, Avro faced challenges that only a handful of aircraft firms had ever faced because it was building an aircraft that operated at twice the speed of sound, just a decade after the first aircraft had broken the sound barrier.

Early in the design process, CF-105 models were tested in wind tunnels, starting with the low-speed

wind tunnel at the National Research Council in
Ottawa. The Arrow required bigger facilities, and so
wind tunnel testing soon shifted across the border to
the Cornell Aeronautical Laboratories in Buffalo, New
York, the facilities of the U.S. National Advisory Committee for Aeronautics (NACA) at Langley Aeronautical Laboratory in Virginia and the Lewis Flight
Propulsion Laboratory in Cleveland, Ohio. Jim Floyd
later estimated that more than 4000 hours of wind
tunnel work went into the Arrow design.

However, wind tunnels couldn't provide answers to
all the questions resulting from the Arrow's new
design and high speeds. Nike rockets topped with
CF-105 models were launched into Lake Ontario at
Point Petre, near Belleville, Ontario. Further launches
took place in the U.S. at the NACA range at Wallops
Island, Virginia, to take advantage of the range's
telemetry facilities. The tests examined the CF-105's
stability, flutter, spin and drag characteristics at subsonic, transonic and supersonic speeds. The launches
also gave the Avro team information about airflow
through the intakes for the Arrow's jet engines. Engineers from Avro, the RCAF and the NRC in Canada,
the RAF in the UK, and NACA and the U.S. Air Force
pored through the data to learn about the Arrow and
high-speed flight in general.

Although Avro and the RCAF received excellent
co-operation from NACA and the U.S. Air Force,
Avro's relationship with the Americans was not without its problems at first. Avro heat transfer engineer
Bryan Erb stated that the RCAF and the NRC became

concerned at one point that the CF-105 would fail to meet projected performance requirements. According to Erb, the RCAF claimed that NACA itself agreed with the gloomy assessment of the Arrow. "The company's response to this was that the wind tunnel data in these NACA reports was okay, but NACA was interpreting it incorrectly, and so was the [RCAF]." When the Avro engineers working on the problem went to the NACA facility at Langley, Virginia, they succeeded in persuading NACA that it was indeed wrong. "This was unprecedented. NACA was the be-all and the end-all of wind tunnel knowledge, and NACA reports were canonical throughout the world. But, as I heard the story, on 20 out of 21 points, the NACA people admitted that the Avro people were right," Erb recalled.

Today, many proud Canadians believe that the Arrow contained many aviation firsts. Although that belief is not borne out by the facts, the design team at Avro did make use of the cutting edge concepts of the day. "We didn't invent anything," Mario Pesando explained. "We exploited it." The notches in the Arrow's delta wings that were required for optimum stability of the aircraft were based on British research. The Arrow's fuselage followed what was known as the "area rule," a concept that gave the fuselage a narrowed "Coke bottle" shape near the wings to allow air to flow around the aircraft at supersonic speeds. According to Pesando, the area rule, which was developed in Germany and refined and popularized by NACA researchers, didn't come to Avro's attention until after development of the Arrow had begun.

To meet the rule's requirements, the Arrow was given a sharper nose cone, a rear fairing and changes in the cross-section of fuselage, which delayed production by several months.

Because they reached such high temperatures, the Arrow's control surfaces had to be constructed of special materials and a powerful air-conditioning system installed inside the aircraft. Sound effects from the engines and from the aerodynamics of supersonic flight put additional strain on the aircraft structure. All these features needed to be tested on the models in wind tunnels and rockets. But the Arrow's designers needed more help to perfect their designs. They turned to a class of devices that, until not long before, was known only in the realm of science fiction: computers.

At first, Avro had a CADAC computer, the first digital computer used by industry in Canada. But the computers of the 1950s were gigantic machines requiring prodigious amounts of power to perform calculations that today can be done with pocket calculators. And those early computers required experts to operate them. To run its new computer, Avro hired Stanley H. Cohn, a mathematician educated at the University of Toronto who had gone to the U.S. to gain experience with the primitive punch-card computers of the time. "They needed a few experienced mathematicians, and preferably with some computer exposure, but since there were no computers in Canada, it was difficult to get computer exposure," Cohn said.

Soon Avro installed an IBM 704 computer, one of the first big, mainframe computers that made IBM famous. The IBM 704 had a memory of a few thousand words, a tiny fraction of today's personal computers' memory but impressive by 1957 standards. The computer was used to do stress analysis and calculations of the Arrow's aerodynamic stability. According to Cohn "You used to do everything in wind tunnels before you had computers, but with computers you could simulate a lot of wind tunnel work so that you would only have to do the refined wind tunnel work." Because the 704 generated a great deal of heat and therefore required its own air-conditioning, the members of Avro's computer department moved from the engineering "bullpen" to the air-conditioned quarters of their computer, something which made their work more bearable in the muggy heat of Toronto summers. The IBM 704 also became a proud symbol of Avro's industrial pre-eminence.

The computers were used to design almost every part of the Arrow, including its complicated landing gear. John Shoosmith, another Avro computer engineer, stated: "We could simulate the motions and figure out the stresses the gear could withstand." The computer was also used to run the Arrow flight simulator and to analyze data obtained during Arrow test flights and recorded on equipment stored in the Arrow's weapons bay.

The Arrow required sophisticated electronic systems. One of these electronic systems constituted a first in a production aircraft, a fly-by-wire control system that transmitted the pilot's stick movements electronically rather than hydraulically or mechanically to the aircraft's control surfaces. This system used an electronic system similar to a computer to help the pilot control the aircraft. At the time, the X-15 rocket plane was the only other aircraft that had a fly-by-wire control system. Up to that time, all aircraft had relied on the direct control inputs of their pilots. Similar systems, which used inputs both from the pilot's controls and from instruments, found their way into all U.S. piloted spacecraft in the 1960s and then into today's high-performance combat aircraft. More recently, fly-by-wire systems have become standard equipment on passenger aircraft.

Perfecting the fly-by-wire system on the Arrow involved a great deal of work by Avro's flight test group throughout the life of the Arrow program and was still unfinished in 1959. Much of this work was done using the Arrow simulator. Tests and estimates of the Arrow's flight characteristics were fed into the simulator by computer to show how the aircraft would react to control inputs by the pilot. A television screen with crude line drawings showed how the aircraft would deal with control inputs at various speeds.

"I learned to fly an airplane, because I thought, if you're going to do flight control systems, you ought to at least know how to fly an airplane," said Richard Carley, a Saskatchewan engineer who helped develop the Arrow's control system on the simulator. "So I was pretty proficient on the simulator." Avro's ace test pilot, Jan Zurakowski, flew the simulator before he took the Arrow into the air for its first flight. Carley remembers Zurakowski being reluctant at first to try the simulator, but soon he became a fan and used it to determine the Arrow's stall characteristics before he flew in the real aircraft.

Avro and Zurakowski had hoped to take the Arrow into the air for the first time in 1957, but the growing complexity and cost of the program was beginning to bring those hopes into question. The year would also bring major surprises that would further affect the fate of the Avro Arrow.

CHAPTER 14

Change of Command

THE LIBERAL CABINET'S apprehensions about the CF-105 program in early 1957 were put aside while its members prepared to go to the hustings in a federal election that was called for June 10. The Liberals had controlled the levers of power in Ottawa since 1935, when Mackenzie King returned to power after Depression-weary voters removed the Conservatives of R.B. Bennett. Until King retired in 1948, his team, which included C.D. Howe, took Canada through the military, political and economic challenges of World War II and the beginnings of the Cold War. Taking his place in the prime minister's chair was Louis St. Laurent, a Québec City lawyer who went on to win two elections in convincing fashion with his avuncular manner.

The decade had seen great economic prosperity, some of it fuelled by the Military Keynesianism of Canada's military buildup after the start of the Korean War. And Avro Canada was at its epicentre. The St. Laurent government improved social programs, including the family allowance or "baby bonus," pensions, federal support for the arts and universities, and public insurance to cover hospital bills, a move that helped lead to the creation of medicare in the 1960s. Further stoking Canadian prosperity and contentment in the 1950s were large infrastructure programs such as the St. Lawrence Seaway, the Trans-Canada Highway and a new pipeline to connect the natural gas fields of Alberta to consumers and factories in eastern Canada. Although Canada had not seen the spectacular communist-hunting congressional hearings of 1950s America, the repressive winds of the Cold War had blown through Canada as well in the form of purges of communists in the civil service and the labour movement.

In 1956, St. Laurent was 74 years old and was beginning to lose interest in politics. He deferred increasingly to Howe, whose impatience with the quarrels of Parliament increased as his time in government went on. The previous year, Howe had attempted to ram a bill through the House of Commons that indefinitely extended his special powers over defence production. The Opposition parties slowed the passage of the bill with lengthy debate, and while Howe was away from Ottawa, St. Laurent finally relented and put a time limit on Howe's powers.

The Trans-Canada Pipeline that was to carry Alberta natural gas to southern Ontario by an all-Canadian route north of Lake Superior had suffered a number of delays by 1956, and Howe was determined to get on with the job. Howe and the government decided to support the American owners of the pipeline company with a major loan and the creation of a Crown corporation that would build part of the pipeline along the bedrock of the Canadian Shield in northern Ontario.

The Cabinet agreed in May to Howe's plan to push the bill through Parliament using closure to restrict debate. This measure, which had not often been used in Parliament up to that time, would ensure that construction could begin that summer, and it would allow Howe to win a measure of revenge for the Opposition's victory the year before with the defence production bill.

The result was one of the legendary episodes of Canadian political history, the Pipeline Debate. The Opposition parties—the Progressive Conservatives and the Co-operative Commonwealth Federation—were determined to renew their attack on the government with an election drawing ever closer. For five weeks, the parties fought over the bill, complete with name-calling, shouting, singing and walkouts. At one point, the Speaker of the House of Commons reversed a ruling that had favoured the Opposition parties, and his decision only inflamed passions. The government eventually prevailed, but the debate had drawn public attention to the arrogance of Howe and the Liberal government.

At the time, the Conservatives were led by George Drew, a former premier of Ontario whose patrician manner fulfilled the stereotype that suspicious voters from other parts of Canada had of him. After losing two elections to St. Laurent, Drew tasted success in the Pipeline Debate, but his health began to trouble him that summer, and he resigned in September. In December, the Tory leadership went to a charismatic lawyer from Saskatchewan named John George Diefenbaker.

John Diefenbaker

The son of a schoolteacher of German descent and a Scots mother, Diefenbaker had finally won a seat in Parliament in 1940 after a long string of political failures. He became a national figure on the Opposition benches and was known for taking on high-profile murder cases as a criminal defence lawyer.

Although Diefenbaker continued to hammer the government in the early months of 1957, few people expected him to beat the mighty Liberal government. But the campaign showed voters that St. Laurent was getting out of touch, and St. Laurent's advanced age made the 61-year-old Diefenbaker look exciting and dynamic. With his fiery eyes, graying hair with black thunderbolt accents and jowls that shook when he was in full oratorical flight, Diefenbaker bore no resemblance to today's television-friendly politicians. But with his ability to stir up crowds and his talent for punchy comments, both honed in the courtroom and his years in politics, Diefenbaker had rare political talent. And in a demanding campaign, Diefenbaker managed to crystallize public opposition to the Liberals and re-establish his party as an acceptable alternative.

When the election took place, Diefenbaker's Progressive Conservative Party won 112 seats in the 265-seat Parliament, seven more than the Liberals, but not a majority. The Conservatives won the seats in and around Malton, and the best-known Liberal defeated that night was C.D. Howe. St. Laurent resigned his office, opening the door for Diefenbaker to become Canada's 13th prime minister.

Because of the Conservatives' long period outside of government, no member of Diefenbaker's Cabinet had previous experience in governing. The new Minister of National Defence was George Pearkes, a British-born soldier who had settled in British Columbia and whose bravery in World War I won him the British Empire's highest award for valour in war, the Victoria

George Pearkes

~~⊙⊃C⊃~~

Cross. Pearkes entered federal politics after a long career in the Canadian Army that ended when he retired as a major general at the end of World War II.

Among the difficult decisions awaiting Diefenbaker and Pearkes were Canada's defence posture and the future of the Arrow program. During the campaign, their Progressive Conservative Party had promised to reduce defence spending. And with his long political career spent in opposition to the Liberals, Diefenbaker had little love for an A.V. Roe Canada that was run by C.D. Howe protégés such as Crawford Gordon and Fred Smye. Like Howe, Diefenbaker and his Cabinet were deeply concerned about the mounting costs of the Arrow, but they were conscious of the economic and military importance of the aircraft. Conservative Members of Parliament from ridings in the Malton area had promised that there would be no layoffs, and every member of the government knew that, with the government in a minority position in Parliament, another election could come at any time.

In September 1957, the new government got a harsh initiation in the politics of dealing with A.V. Roe Canada. When the government decided not to proceed with the Mark VI version of the CF-100, Avro informed the government that nearly 3000 employees would be laid off. Labour Minister Michael Starr told Cabinet that he thought Avro "was adopting a vindictive attitude and that in their lay-offs they were going far beyond what was necessary." Cabinet discussed the matter three times within a week and finally decided to reduce the need for layoffs by building additional Mark V CF-100s. Avro anxiously awaited word on the future of the Arrow, and Cabinet agreed to extend the Arrow program by a year, but the program was put under review. Cabinet confirmed the existing order of 29 pre-production Arrows on top of the eight prototypes then being built. The Diefenbaker government had had little time to study the Arrow program, and it had little room to manoeuver because of its precarious minority position. Soon the government would find itself in an even more awkward position as the Arrow became a reality and a new age of warfare suddenly began.

CHAPTER 15

Rollout

AVRO CHOSE THE FIRST Friday of October for the official unveiling of the first completed Avro Arrow, and the company pulled out all the stops to create a memorable event. At 2:30 PM in the sunshine, the event began with the RCAF band playing for more than 10,000 people who stood before the decorated hangar and speaker's platform at the Malton plant. On the platform were two dozen dignitaries including Crawford Gordon of Avro, Sir Roy Dobson of the Hawker Siddeley Group, U.S. Air Force General Leon Johnson and John A. D. McCurdy.

Fred Smye began the formalities by introducing the star of the show, which was still inside the hangar. "The Avro Arrow is a twin-engine, long-range, day-and-night supersonic interceptor. It has a crew of two. It is a big, versatile aircraft. The primary armament of the aircraft is to be air-to-air guided missiles installed in a detachable armament bay in the fuselage. The versatility provided by this armament will enable the aircraft to perform other roles. The aircraft will be equipped with one of the most advanced integrated electronics systems, which will combine the navigation and operation of the aircraft with its fire-control system."

After Smye expressed the hope that the Arrow would fly before the end of the year, RCAF Air Marshal Hugh L. Campbell, Chief of the Air Staff, took the podium. "Suffice to say the planned performance of this aircraft is such that it can effectively meet and deal with any likely bomber threat to this continent over the next decade. We in the air force look upon this aircraft as one component of a complex and elaborate air defence system covering in the first instance the whole of the North American continent, extending from Labrador to Hudson Bay to the Queen Charlotte Islands," he said.

Campbell spoke of the Arrow's role in defending a perimeter that extended from Alaska to Turkey against the West's Cold War adversary, the Soviet Union, and he highlighted the effort that had brought about the Arrow.

"There are many difficult problems ahead," he went on. "Some can be foreseen, but some are hidden by the veil covering the unknown areas of aerodynamic science, which has still to be explored."

Finally, the headline speaker stood up and gave his speech. George Pearkes, the Minister of National Defence, ended his remarks by pulling on a golden rope that hung next to the lectern where he stood. With that, a curtain in the door of the hangar bearing the words "Avro Arrow" parted, and a white tractor slowly pulled out a white jet aircraft with two engines

The first Arrow surrounded by crowds on rollout day, October 4, 1957

and delta wings, a swept-back rudder and a black nose. The band struck up a fanfare and the "RCAF March Past" while CF-100 aircraft flew overhead.

The flypast gained only momentary attention as those in the crowd strained to get a better look at the aircraft rolling out of the hangar. The sleek, gleaming white CF-105 was more than 24 metres long, with a wingspan of 15 metres and a weight of 22 tonnes, without the fuel for its two engines.

The thousands of people who had turned out for the ceremony were soon able to surround the CF-105 Avro Arrow, and in the excitement, most probably forgot what Pearkes had just said.

"Much has been said of late about the coming missile age," the minister stated. "And there have been suggestions from well-intentioned people that the era of the manned aeroplane is over and that we should not be wasting our time and energy producing an aircraft of the performance, complexity and cost of the Avro Arrow. They suggest that we should put our faith in missiles and launch straight into an era of push-button war. I do not feel that missile and manned aircraft have, as yet, reached the point where they should be considered competitive. They will, in fact, become complementary. However, the aircraft has this one great advantage over the missile. It can bring the judgement of a man into the battle and closer to the target where human judgement, combined with the technology of the aircraft, will provide the most sophisticated and effective defence that human ingenuity can devise.

"The aircraft now being produced in the various countries of our NATO alliance may or may not be the last of the manned interceptors. With the rapid strides being made in the fields of science and engineering, it would be unwise to attempt to forecast the future in this respect."

No one who took part in the ceremony that afternoon had any idea of how soon those words would be put to the test.

CHAPTER 16

Sputnik

AFTER THE CEREMONY, while many of the workers and other interested onlookers went home, the management of Avro Canada and their honoured guests retired to Briarcrest, which was stocked for a celebration planned for late afternoon and into the evening. Bob Lindley was driving two USAF generals back to the airport from the celebration when news came over their car radio that the Soviet Union had just launched an artificial satellite into orbit around the Earth. The satellite, which the Soviets announced was called *Sputnik*, or "fellow traveller," had gone into space before the Americans could launch their own, giving the Soviets the first victory in the Space Race between the two Cold War adversaries.

Sputnik's launch was also an unmistakable sign that the Soviet Union possessed intercontinental ballistic missiles (ICBM) that could shoot nuclear weapons from the Russian heartland to targets in the U.S. and Canada in a matter of minutes. The "missile age" and the era of "push-button war" that Pearkes had talked about just hours earlier had suddenly arrived. And to the astonishment of everyone outside the communist

Sputnik

~∞X∞~

world who heard the news, the Russians were ahead of the United States.

The reaction in Lindley's car to the news that evening was being replicated all across Canada and the U.S. Until they could confirm the news, no one in the car believed that the Soviets had launched a satellite before the Americans. "I knew the Russians meant business," Lindley recalled later. "They destroyed our rollout."

Bryan Erb, who had also taken in the rollout, heard the news on his home radio. "It was a collective feeling that the aeronautical community had done it," Erb recalled thinking at the time. "The fact that it was the

Russians didn't matter. It completely overwhelmed the Arrow rollout in significance for the day."

The wholly unexpected news of that October evening had its roots in the events that marked the end of World War II and the beginning of the Cold War. The German invasion of 1941 and the battles that brought German armies to the gates of Moscow, Leningrad and Stalingrad ended with the Soviet hammer and sickle flag flying over Berlin. More than 25 million Soviet citizens died during that time. The Soviet dictator, Josef Stalin, was determined to prevent a repeat of the war, and he installed puppet regimes in the Eastern European countries occupied by Soviet troops. The spread of communist regimes in Europe, and later in China, brought fears that Soviet expansionism would spread further.

The Gouzenko affair had been the first tangible evidence of the massive Soviet effort to acquire Western military secrets, especially the atomic bomb. The data picked up by Soviet spies during and after the war was combined with the work of Soviet nuclear physicists to create the first Soviet atomic bomb in 1949 and a more powerful hydrogen bomb four years later.

Although the Soviet nuclear feats were impressive, the Soviets needed more to have a credible nuclear force. They had nuclear weapons, but they still needed the means to deliver the bombs to their targets. The American B-29s that carried the first atomic bombs to Hiroshima and Nagasaki were far more advanced than any aircraft in the Soviet arsenal, and even a B-29 could not carry nuclear weapons from the Soviet Union to the United States. Stalin had ordered the aircraft designers who had survived the war and the terror he and his security forces had unleashed on millions of Soviet citizens in the 1930s to replicate the B-29 and then set to work on bigger bombers that could threaten the U.S. The work of building aircraft that could fly thousands of kilometres from Russia to America proved to be more difficult than expected. And while the U.S. had allies ringing the Soviet Union that allowed the Americans to place bombers close to the Soviet frontiers, the Russians did not have a similar advantage. By the mid-1950s, Stalin was dead and Soviet aircraft designers were coming up with bombers that made the Americans nervous. But Stalin had not left the delivery problem purely in the hands of his aircraft people. The war had showed him the possibilities offered by the rocket.

In the 1930s, the German army had embarked on a massive effort to build missiles that could threaten their enemies. They had hired rocket enthusiasts such as Wernher von Braun and other engineers and brought them together to build the V-2, a rocket that could deliver a one-tonne warhead nearly 300 kilometres. The program proceeded in fits and starts because of Hitler's mixed feelings about the rocket and Britain's bombing of the German rocket development site. Finally, in September 1944, the V-2 began being used against targets in Britain and liberated Belgium and France.

The V-2 represented a major advance in rocketry, but its poor accuracy and its deployment late in the war limited its effectiveness to the point where twice as many people died building the rockets in factories staffed with concentration camp inmates than were killed by V-2 attacks. When the war came to an end, American, British, French and Soviet forces scooped up the engineers and scientists who had designed and built the V-2, and they also grabbed the remaining rockets and associated parts and equipment. The U.S. Army managed to acquire most of the leading designers, including von Braun, and most of the rockets. Both the people and the rockets were shipped to the White Sands testing range in New Mexico, where von Braun's team worked with American experts on scientific test launches of the V-2. But the Americans did not embark on an aggressive missile development effort of their own at the time because they felt secure with their nuclear monopoly and their bombers.

The Soviet effort to obtain the rocket and its designers was less successful than the American effort, but the Soviets were able to hire a group of German rocket engineers and a few V-2s to test and launch. At first, they worked in laboratories in the parts of Germany occupied by Soviet forces, but in 1946, they were suddenly moved to a laboratory near Moscow. Stalin had ordered his own rocket engineers to replicate the V-2 and then build bigger rockets that could carry nuclear weapons over the pole to targets in the United States. The Soviet rocket effort came under the leadership of Sergei Korolev, who had survived Stalin's prison camps during the Great Terror of the late 1930s and then established himself as the leader of the Soviet missile effort after the war. The Germans were sent home from Russia once the Soviets were satisfied that they had gained all the knowledge they could from their guests, and Korolev's efforts culminated in a rocket the Soviets called the R-7.

The R-7 flew for the first time in May 1957, but as with many missile tests, this flight ended in failure not far from the launch pad that had been built in an isolated part of Kazakhstan. After another failure, the R-7 flew true on August 21, sending a warhead near its target thousands of kilometres away. When the Soviet news agency TASS announced the success a few days later, it won attention in the West, but any alarm was muted by skepticism about the Soviet claim. Similar reactions had greeted the Soviet announcement two years earlier that they planned to launch a satellite, as well as their announcements in the summer of 1957 about the radio frequencies to be used by the satellite.

Once the R-7 had flown successfully, Soviet leaders gave Korolev the go-ahead to launch a satellite. Finally, on the evening of October 4, Korolev and his team launched *Sputnik*. Once the satellite's orbit had been confirmed, TASS announced the success to a stupefied world. The next day's edition of the official Soviet newspaper, *Pravda,* carried the news of *Sputnik*'s launch as a routine report. But newspapers and other media outside the Soviet Union treated *Sputnik*'s launch as a world-shaking event. Canadian papers gave *Sputnik* the headlines that would otherwise have gone to the newly unveiled Arrow.

Congratulations began pouring into Moscow, to the delight and surprise of Soviet Premier Nikita Khrushchev. The following day's *Pravda* picked up on this response and, like every other newspaper, gave *Sputnik* banner headlines across page one. The Soviets moved quickly to exploit this propaganda triumph by pointing to the satellite as proof of communism's superiority to capitalism. People around the world paused to watch *Sputnik* pass overhead in the evening or pre-dawn skies, while radio hobbyists worked to pick up its beeping signal.

Khrushchev wanted another space success, and so on November 3, Korolev and his team launched *Sputnik 2*, which was substantially heavier than the first *Sputnik* and carried a live passenger, a mongrel dog named Laika. Although Laika died in space because her satellite had no recovery system, her flight sent a clear signal that the Soviet Union was thinking of launching a human passenger. The fact that the Soviets could orbit a heavy satellite carrying a dog also emphasized the fact to nervous Americans that the Soviets had missiles that could drop nuclear bombs anywhere on Earth.

～❀～

go, Gordon put Fred Smye in charge of the aircraft division and brought in new people to run the engine division. Under this new structure, the problems with the CF-100 were solved, and production of the aircraft and the Orenda engine were accelerated to meet Howe's demands.

By 1954, Gordon had the CF-100 production going smoothly, the Jetliner program closed down and engineers hard at work designing the successor to the CF-100. For the new aircraft, he was determined to avoid the problems that had plagued the CF-100, one of which was dependence on outside contractors. "During the war, C.D. Howe had taught Gordon a basic principle of production—control your source of supply," Stewart wrote. Gordon also wanted to diversify the company so that it was not solely dependent on building aircraft for the Canadian government. The aircraft and engine divisions became separate companies, with the aircraft division named Avro Aircraft Ltd. and the engine division named after its major product, the Orenda engine. In December, Avro purchased Canadian Steel Improvement, which supplied turbine blades for aircraft engines. In 1955, Avro took over Canadian Car and Foundry, which produced railway equipment, buses, trailers, aircraft and various other products. Gordon took Avro public the next year and used the capital he raised to purchase more companies, including Canadian Applied Research Ltd., a stake in Algoma Steel and, finally, control of Canada's third largest steel maker, the Nova Scotia based Dominion Steel and Coal Corporation (Dosco).

CHAPTER 17

The Americans Respond

THE AMERICAN RESPONSE to *Sputnik* was what one historian described as a "media riot" that led to questions about the U.S. missile and space programs. On the day *Sputnik* was launched, America had no ICBM flying and no satellite in orbit. Reporters and politicians demanded to know why, and President Dwight D. Eisenhower tried to calm the storm, though his hands were tied by the fact that much of the knowledge he had was classified and couldn't be shared with the public.

In the early days of the Cold War, the U.S. government had not pushed ahead with rocket or satellite programs because of their strong position at the time. But once the Soviets exploded their first atomic bomb, attitudes began to change. The communist takeover of China and the start of the Korean War caused the U.S. government to massively increase funding for weapons systems such as missiles.

Wernher von Braun and his German rocket team moved from the desert to an army installation at Huntsville, Alabama, where they were put to work on the Redstone, a missile that could launch weapons over intermediate distances. In 1951, a San Diego aircraft contractor, Convair, won a contract to work on ICBM concepts, and after Eisenhower took office in 1953, the air force was directed to accelerate work on Convair's missile, which became known as the Atlas. The project involved a massive management effort under USAF General Bernard Schriever, but the first Atlas exploded on the launch pad in June 1957. The Atlas team had a series of problems to overcome before the missile successfully flew in November 1958, giving America its first operational ICBM soon afterwards.

The air force was focused on developing its missile and not on space. But American scientists were aiming to put satellites into orbit in 1957 and 1958 as part of a worldwide research effort known as the International Geophysical Year (IGY). Proposals were already being floated for satellites in the early 1950s, and Eisenhower hoped that a satellite could be developed that could photograph closed-off areas of the Soviet Union and provide rare and precious information on the strength of its military, especially its nuclear forces. By launching a scientific satellite as part of the IGY, Eisenhower and his administration hoped to establish the right of overflight by satellites, and so in 1955, the White House announced the launch. To the surprise of many people, the Soviet Union responded days later with a similar announcement of their own.

As early as 1956, von Braun's team had been working on an upgraded version of the Redstone, called Jupiter C, with extra stages that they believed could launch a satellite into orbit, but a government committee chose to go with another proposal called Vanguard that involved the creation of a new rocket and satellite under the auspices of the U.S. Navy. Vanguard faced its own set of delays and challenges, and so the Soviets won the honour of launching the first satellite.

After the setbacks to American pride caused by the first two *Sputnik*s, Americans were shocked when they watched the first U.S. rocket launch, televised live on December 6, end with the explosion of a Vanguard test vehicle and its satellite. The White House, desperate for a success, freed von Braun and his team to prepare a Jupiter C for launch. On January 31, 1958, the first U.S. satellite, Explorer I, was put into orbit.

The launch showed that the Americans were still in the Space Race, and the success of the Atlas missile later in the year pulled the U.S. even, and then ahead, of the Soviet Union in the missile race. But this left open the question of where defensive systems such as the Avro Arrow fit in the new strategic equation.

~eᗡᑕᘎ~

CHAPTER 18

Defensive Doctrines

THE LAUNCH OF *SPUTNIK* raised the spectre of push-button wars with missiles and again raised the question of the usefulness of the Arrow. The question was a long-standing one. Before the Korean War, Canada's defence policy had been based on the North Atlantic alliance that found its expression in NATO. But, as James Dow argued in his book, after the war, Canada was left to find a place in a new environment in which the U.S. promised massive nuclear retaliation in case of attack. "Canada's failure to establish a clear national direction for defence policy after the Korean War left Avro in a strategic limbo," Dow wrote. "Where the CF-100 had been conceived as a fighter whose primary purpose was to guard Canada from air attack, the Arrow's main task would be to help shield the American strategic deterrent."

A few weeks after taking office in the summer of 1957, Prime Minister Diefenbaker and Defence Minister Pearkes decided that Canada would join the United States in the North American Air Defence Command (NORAD). The decision was based on work done by the former Liberal government and the RCAF and included the integration of operational command of air forces to protect both countries against Soviet attack over the pole. The Liberals had already given the U.S. Air Force the right of interception over Canadian air space, and Canada was dotted with radar stations. The outgoing government had refused to complete the NORAD agreement in March for fear of controversy in the election campaign, and as the Chief of the Defence Staff admitted years later, he and his military colleagues "stampeded" Diefenbaker and Pearkes into agreeing to NORAD that summer. They had agreed to join NORAD, a decision that is still in effect today, without even consulting the Cabinet Defence Committee or Cabinet. The new command would be based in Colorado Springs, Colorado, with an American commander and a Canadian deputy. It was only later that Diefenbaker learned the full implications of this decision.

The Liberals had declined to deal head on with the issue of Canada's defence relationship with the U.S., and by quickly signing on to NORAD without considering the full implications of the unified command, so had the new Conservative government. For the time being, the move to NORAD made both countries jointly responsible for the defence of Canada's airspace against Soviet bombers. And as Dow suggested, this meant that supporters of the Arrow were defending the integration of American and Canadian air defences while arguing for the autonomy of Canada's defence industry.

Sputnik caused the basic strategic questions to be asked again, and for the next few years, debates raged about the need for bombers versus ICBMs, and consequently the need for interceptor aircraft such as the Arrow. In the wake of *Sputnik*, both sides moved much of their nuclear arsenals to ICBMs and submarine-launched ballistic missiles, but they also kept their nuclear-armed bombers. Even with the retention of bombers, the arrival of ICBMs raised the question of how much money should be spent on systems such as the CF-105, when the threat of bombers was fading in the face of the move to missiles.

The previous April, Duncan Sandys, the British Minister of Defence, produced a White Paper that was based on the assumption that missiles would replace bomber aircraft. The result was the cancellation of most British combat aircraft under development at the time in favour of work on missile programs. Although some of Sandys' decisions were later reversed, they led to the consolidation of the British aircraft industry, and in the short term, more British workers becoming available for work at Avro Canada. The British aircraft programs would not be the only casualties as defence programs shifted away from bombers and toward missiles and deterrence.

~∞~

CHAPTER 19

First Flight

WITHIN A FEW DAYS of the Arrow's rollout, the RCAF made the long overdue decision to set up an Arrow project office under Group Captain Ray Footit, who during his RCAF career had been involved with the Arrow from its inception. "One lesson that came out of World War II was that you had to have project management," Footit said later. "Project management is now something everybody knows and everybody does, but within the air force in the early days, it was all parcelled out in different directorates and with different people doing different things." Footit said he had previously opposed moves to arm the Arrow with the latest weapons, and now he was faced with the consequences of those decisions in the form of a new cost estimate for the Arrow program. "We came up with a figure of about a billion dollars, and nobody had ever looked at that kind of figure before." With the Arrow officially under review, the number sent chills around Ottawa and Malton.

Meanwhile, work at Avro continued on preparing for the first flight of the CF-105. Fred Smye's hope for a flight in 1957 was dashed while the first Arrow underwent tests and preparations for its first flight.

This work focused on the Pratt and Whitney engines, along with the Arrow's landing gear and brakes. The main landing gear required thorough testing because it had to fit inside the thin delta wings of the Arrow, and to do so, it rotated and shortened as it folded up. The ground test department oversaw testing of the Arrow's Martin-Baker ejection seat, and the whole plant was invited to watch a test firing of the seat with a dummy on board. The test was successful, and a tether and net attached to the equipment ensured that the seat and the dummy could be used another day rather than being destroyed in the fall. To test how well and what pilots would see during the Arrow's takeoffs and landings, a full-scale model of the Arrow's cockpit was mounted on a stand on the back of a flatbed truck that was driven on the runway.

Tests of the first Arrow's engines were conducted in December, and the following month, the Arrow began taxi trials, in which Janusz Zurakowski ran the aircraft up and down the runway to test its handling before takeoff and after landing. The taxi tests included runs with the drag chute, and they uncovered problems with the brakes. The first set of brakes was inadequate and needed to be replaced with stronger ones. In the early tests, the heat generated by the braking caused the drums to turn white hot and heat the rims, bursting the tires. Zurakowski ran from the aircraft after some taxi tests to avoid bursting tires.

Once, the Avro flight test department had a fire truck spread water on the tarmac on a cold February day to make sure that the anti-skid brakes worked as advertised. "My most vivid memory is of the high-speed landing brake tests," said Peter Armitage, who helped run the tests. "I would dash out with a hand pyrometer to measure brake temperature. Only later on, with a more safety-conscious mind, did I realize how dangerous that was. The tire pressures were 400 pounds per square inch, and if one had blown—goodbye career!"

Zurakowski and other pilots scheduled to fly the Arrow were also preparing for their flights by "flying" the Arrow flight simulator, in which they could test the aircraft in various simulated situations. The pilots pronounced themselves satisfied with the experience they gained in the simulator.

Finally, in March 1958, the Arrow was nearly ready to take to the skies. Hopes of a March 22 flight were dashed when a hydraulic leak caused the flight to be postponed. Three days later, the public address system in the Avro plant announced that the first Arrow flight was ready to go, and that non-essential personnel could go outside and watch. The plant emptied quickly as Zurakowski made his final inspection of the first Arrow, RL201, signed his acceptance and climbed the ladder to the cockpit. He started the engines and taxied the Arrow onto runway 32. Two chase aircraft—a CF-100 piloted by Avro test pilot "Spud" Potocki and an F-86 with RCAF test pilot Jack Woodman at the controls—were in the air when Zurakowski and RL201 took to the air at 9:51 AM.

Zurakowski closed the landing gear and had Potocki inspect the nose wheel door when a light in his cockpit indicated that it hadn't closed. Zurakowski then flew the Arrow in a set of non-demanding manoeuvers to test the aircraft's handling. Thirty-five minutes after takeoff, Zurakowski lowered the landing gear and touched ground. After taxiing the aircraft back to the plant and shutting down the engines, Zurakowski descended from the cockpit and was lifted on the shoulders of jubilant workers.

He later reported that the Avro handled in a manner similar to other delta-winged aircraft, such as the Gloster Javelin from Britain or the American F-102. He recorded that only two microswitches failed to work, and that the aircraft responded in a similar manner to the simulator, an important finding for the expensive and complicated device that was training future pilots for the Arrow.

Even before that day, Zurakowski's flying career had become something of a legend. He had been born in 1914 to Polish parents in what was then Russian territory and today is part of Ukraine. He was brought up in Poland after it regained its independence, and during his childhood, he dreamed of becoming a fighter pilot. He made his first flight at age 15, and when he finished high school, he learned how to fly. Zurakowski soon joined the Polish armed forces and furthered his pilot's training. By the time war broke out in 1939, he was an instructor in the Polish air force. Zurakowski flew combat missions when the Germans invaded, but he and other members of the Polish air force were forced to escape when Soviet armies moved in to claim their part of Poland under the terms of the infamous

The first Avro Arrow in flight

Nazi-Soviet Non-Aggression Pact. Zurakowski fled through Romania and the Middle East and made his way to France and then Britain. He joined a Polish Squadron in the RAF, flying a Spitfire in the Battle of Britain in 1940 and continuing to fly during the war.

After the war ended and Soviet forces occupied his beloved Poland, Zurakowski enrolled in the Empire Test Pilots' School and flew the RAF's latest aircraft. He joined the Gloster Aircraft company and test flew their famed Meteor, one of the world's first operational jet aircraft. He became famous flying the Meteor at the 1951 Farnborough Air Show with a cartwheel manoeuver that became known as the "Zurabatic Cartwheel." The next year Zurakowski accepted a test flying position at Avro Canada and moved his family to his new adopted country. At Avro, he mastered the CF-100 and, in 1958, gained fame by being the first to fly the Arrow. His aviation career was now tied to the aircraft that had made him famous.

CHAPTER 20

The Northern Vision

THE DIEFENBAKER GOVERNMENT had to tread carefully in 1957 because it did not hold a majority of seats in the House of Commons. But after getting over the surprise of turning out the Liberals after so many years, Canadians were happily embracing their new Conservative government in a prolonged political honeymoon. Diefenbaker was sorely tempted to ask for a dissolution of Parliament and a new election, but he held back. Among those who were urging him to call a quick election was his defence minister, George Pearkes, who wrote him with a warning that hard decisions involving "radical changes" would have to be made in 1958. "For instance, it is not at all clear that we need to proceed with the construction of the CF-105," Pearkes wrote. "If next summer we have to cancel development of this aircraft, the aircraft industry at the Avro plant will be seriously dislocated with possible large-scale layoffs of personnel."

Meanwhile, St. Laurent and Howe both decided to leave public life, and the Liberal Party held a leadership convention in January 1958, in which the former external affairs minister, Lester B. (Mike) Pearson, defeated veteran Cabinet minister Paul Martin, father of the future prime minister. Pearson had distinguished himself as a diplomat before entering politics, and his work in arranging for peacekeeping forces following the 1956 war in the Middle East won him the 1957 Nobel Peace Prize.

On January 20, Pearson took his seat in the House of Commons for the first time as Leader of the Opposition and made a gigantic political mistake that made the day one of the most dramatic in Canadian Parliamentary history. Pearson stood up to speak on a routine motion to vote money for government operations, a motion that if defeated would bring down the government. Pearson strongly criticized the Conservative government's economic policies and said an election would worsen Canada's economic situation. Then in a move that shocked both sides of the House, Pearson called for a government that would "implement Liberal policies," and called on the Diefenbaker government to resign, clearing the way for a return of the Liberals without an election.

Diefenbaker and his Conservative colleagues could scarcely believe their luck at such a demonstration of arrogance from the Liberal Party's new leader. The prime minister stood up and responded with one of the greatest performances of his political career. Diefenbaker took apart his political adversaries in a two-hour speech that he capped by revealing a "hidden report" prepared for the former government before the 1957 election that forecast economic trouble ahead. Paul Martin called it "one of the greatest devastating speeches" in Canadian history. Diefenbaker now had the pretext he needed, and on February 1, the governor general called an election for March 31.

Diefenbaker then embarked on a campaign that was extraordinary by any standard. Everywhere the prime minister went, he was greeted by large and rapturous crowds, while the Liberals and other parties drew little interest from the public. Diefenbaker campaigned in front of excited crowds on an undefined "vision" of Canada. He refined the themes of his 1957 campaign, speaking of his "vision" of riches from the unknown and untapped resources in Canada's northern territories. He promised "roads to resources" in the North and aid to Canada's farmers, but he didn't talk about the Avro Arrow. Although he spoke virtually no French, Diefenbaker had won the support of Québec's premier, Maurice Duplessis, who deployed his legendary political machine on behalf of the Conservatives. On March 31, 1958, Diefenbaker won an unprecedented total of 208 seats in the 264-seat House of Commons, a victory that has been matched on only one occasion since. His victory, just six days after the first flight of the Avro Arrow, gave him the freedom to make decisions on many issues, including the fate of the Arrow.

~∞~

CHAPTER 21

Test Flying the Arrow

WHILE OTHER CANADIANS were absorbing the results the day after the 1958 federal election, Jan Zurakowski flew the Arrow on its second test flight, which was cut short when the nose wheel failed to retract. Two days later, however, Zurakowski took the Arrow above the speed of sound for the first time. When Zurakowski flew the Arrow on its 11th flight in June, the landing gear on the port wing failed to engage properly, and the aircraft skidded off the runway, causing some damage. The aircraft was grounded until October, and Arrow test flights did not resume until August, when the second Arrow was ready to fly. The flight-test program continued into fall and winter, with the third Arrow taking to the air in October, the fourth in November and the fifth in January.

The Arrow's eighth flight had someone new at the controls: RCAF Flight Lieutenant Jack Woodman. A native of Saskatoon, Woodman joined the RCAF in the war and served in combat in Europe as a gunner. After his discharge at the war's end, Woodman went to engineering school and rejoined the RCAF in 1948, quickly earning his pilot's wings. In 1951, he attended the Empire Test Pilots' School in England and became an RCAF test pilot, working on the CF-100 program. He later helped the USAF team that tested the F-102, which provided him with both the supersonic and delta-wing experience that would help him fly the Arrow as an RCAF project pilot.

"The airplane, at certain speeds and altitudes, flew as well as any airplane I've ever flown; at other points, control was very sensitive and the airplane difficult to fly accurately," Woodman recalled years later. "However, I know that it was just a matter of optimizing the controls, the damping system and the feel throughout the complete flight envelope. And it would have been accomplished."

One of the Arrow's most innovative design features was its weapons pack, which formed an integral part of the lower fuselage. Self-contained weapons packs carrying different weapons could be changed quickly between flights, and one pack could be recharged while another pack featuring the same or different weapons was fastened to the aircraft for another flight. The weapons, in most cases missiles, would remain inside the pack until they were required and would not impart drag to the aircraft until moments before they were fired.

The idea behind the weapons pack came from Bob Lindley, who decided to make a virtue out of necessity. Because the exact weapons the Arrow would carry remained in question, placing the weapons inboard inside the weapons pack allowed the Arrow design team to get on with designing and building the aircraft without having to make changes every time the weapons changed. The weapons pack also would have allowed different types of weapons to be introduced without having to make other changes on the aircraft. There would, of course, be design work for the weapons' deployment systems.

During the test program, the weapons packs were replaced with instrument packs containing equipment that recorded data on the aircraft's performance in flight. Woodman later said that the flight test instrumentation system "was a constant source of trouble during the Arrow program. During the first series of flights, the system was plagued with a number of problems that were probably due to the thousands of wires and connections running to the instrument pack. But as I remember, these problems were never really resolved, and many a flight was delayed because of this system."

The equipment in the instrument packs was run by the electronics group in Avro's flight test department. A member of this group, George Harris Jr., an engineer from Britain, recalled that 2.5-centimetre magnetic tape, then a new medium, was used inside the aircraft to record data. The systems were tested in a CF-100 before being used in the Arrow, and the magnetic tape had the benefit of being compatible with the IBM 704 computer. But there was also a need for data to be provided live to the ground. So 11 strip chart recorders were set up in the control centre to record the eight channels of data that came from the aircraft. In the centre of the room sat the one person who could talk to the pilot. Harris said the setup was called the High Speed Flight Centre. "We could look at it with some kind of pride because, to our knowledge, it was the first one of its kind that anybody had put together in North America."

The information obtained from these recorders was not only used to assess how the aircraft was standing up to the stresses it was under, or to compare flight data to wind tunnel and rocket data; it was also used to help pilots prepare for flight. Once the aircraft began flying, the Arrow simulator used actual flight data to verify that the simulator's performance matched the characteristics of the aircraft. As well, data from the flights were played back through the computer into the simulator to see what outputs appeared on the control panel.

As the flight-test program continued, two other Avro test pilots began to fly the Arrow. Waldeck (Spud) Potocki, who, like Zurakowski, was Polish, also served in the RAF during the war and attended the Empire Test Pilots' School before finding work at Avro Canada. Peter Cope was born in England and joined the RAF at the start of the war, flying photo-reconnaissance missions over England. After attending the Empire Test Pilots' School, he worked as a test pilot at the Armstrong-Whitworth Company in England before joining Avro Canada in 1951.

Zurakowski took the second and third Arrows up for their first flights. After flying the first three Arrows a total of 21 times and spending nearly 24 hours in the air in the CF-105, Zurakowski retired from the ranks of test pilots at the end of September 1958. Then, at age 44, he became a staff engineer at Avro.

Potocki flew the Arrow more than anyone else did and was the only pilot to fly all five completed Arrows. He reported that most of his flights on the Arrow went smoothly, with occasional problems with the brakes and burst tires, or a drag chute that refused to deploy. However, one flight caused him fear when the Arrow began to fly violently and independently of his inputs to the control system in fly-by-wire. After the plane porpoised a few times, Potocki switched the control system to manual and brought the plane under control.

On November 11, 1958, Potocki took Arrow 202 up for the 44th flight of the program—a flight that turned out to be memorable in more than one way. That day, Potocki took the Arrow out to Lake Superior and then turned it around and flew towards Ottawa in a speed run at Mach 1.98, just under twice the speed of sound. Potocki was under strict orders to not fly the aircraft any faster, and like a good test pilot, he followed those orders.

In Avro's High Speed Flight Centre, the rule was that only one person could talk to the pilot, and for most flights, including this one, an ex-wing commander from the RAF served as the aircraft communicator. Fred Matthews, a member of the test team, said the single point of contact was used "to keep the babble of engineers from talking to the pilot and confusing the issue." The centre was hooked up to a radar operator at an air defence radar station in Orillia, about 100 kilometres north of Toronto. Although the radar operator couldn't talk to the pilot, his voice could be heard on loudspeakers. He was only supposed to speak if there was a traffic problem or if the Arrow pilot needed a fix on his location.

The day Potocki took the Arrow on its run to the edge of Mach 2, the radar operator, who Matthews believed had never seen anything on his screen move faster than the subsonic CF-100, couldn't suppress himself. "Will you look at that sonofabitch go!" the operator yelled over the control centre loudspeakers. "Will you look at that sonofabitch go!" Added Matthews: "We never did find out how fast the airplane could go. It was still accelerating and still climbing, and that was with the J-75 engine and not the Iroquois engine. They never did find out how fast it could go."

The drama of the day was not over. When Potocki turned back to Malton to bring the Arrow home, he sensed as he touched down that he had no brakes. In such circumstances, he would normally take off again and try another landing, but his fuel was low after the record-setting run, and he continued to land. He later learned that the brakes had locked, and that the heat generated in the brakes eventually burned through the brake drums, causing the tires to explode. "I lost control of the aircraft, which swung to the right off the runway. The right main gear collapsed, and I came to a grinding halt with my right wing tip dragging on the ground." The surprised pilot got out of the cockpit and walked down the wing and off the aircraft. The landing problem was later traced to the settings on the Arrow's elevators, which regulate the amount of lift given by its wings. This was the second and final landing mishap with the CF-105.

Many reports gave the Arrow top marks on its flying characteristics, but aviation author Larry Milberry assessed Potocki's pilot's handling notes about the Arrow and noted that Potocki made frequent references to handling problems, especially sideslip. "The Arrow was a challenge from the start, and far from a piece of cake to fly," Milberry wrote in *Canada's Air Force at War and Peace*. "Naturally, through cautious, step-by-step testing, most such shortcomings would have been rectified, but others would have caused costly delays."

The Arrow's flight-test program continued as the year came to an end, but because of problems far away from the flight line, the Arrow program was encountering more political problems than ever.

CHAPTER 22

Storm Clouds Gather

EVEN AS THE AVRO ARROW flight-test program was still in its early days in the spring of 1958, political storm clouds had gathered over the aircraft. First, the huge majority Diefenbaker won on election night in 1958 gave him a free hand to deal with issues such as the Arrow program. The prime minister was known for keeping political grudges, and the animus he and other Conservatives felt for C.D. Howe was especially powerful. Diefenbaker and Pearkes were also well aware of Howe's concerns about the Arrow program and other problems he had encountered at Avro Canada.

The news heralded by *Sputnik* that the Soviet Union possessed ICBMs threw U.S. and Canadian defence planning into confusion. The boasts of Soviet Premier Nikita Khrushchev that the Soviet Union was turning out ICBMs "like sausages" and that bombers were obsolete were widely believed until photos from U-2 spy planes and reconnaissance satellites disproved them. But in 1958, many defence experts believed that the days of the nuclear bomber were numbered, and that defence strategy should turn to dealing with the ICBM threat. Aircraft programs in the United States and elsewhere in the non-communist world were being shut down as militaries shifted resources toward missiles.

This question tied in to an even greater political problem for the Arrow. Canadian military leaders were beginning to shy away from the aircraft as its costs grew. By the end of March of that year, the Arrow's costs had exceeded $100 million without even counting the costs of the Iroquois engine, the Sparrow missile or the Astra electronic control system. Although Air Marshall Hugh Campbell, the RCAF Chief of Staff, continued to support the Arrow, the leaders of the Canadian army and navy began to turn against it. Historians Russell Isinger and Donald C. Story wrote: "One must keep in mind at this time the Royal Canadian Air Force, the premier service, was allotted almost 50 percent of the defence budget, and interservice rivalry had been simmering for years as [Chiefs of Staff Committee Chair General Charles] Foulkes and the navy and the army chiefs realized that, if the Arrow program went ahead as planned, there would be little money to replace aging frigates or to acquire new armoured vehicles and tactical nuclear missiles."

According to Dow, the Chiefs of Staff were considering three options for the Arrow. One was cancellation of the program, the second was building 100 Arrows, and the third was ending the program after the 37 aircraft already on order were built. If the third option were chosen, Canada would have to consider buying the new and highly advanced Bomarc Surface-to-Air Missiles. "But this would give the air force a missile of only limited effectiveness and burden it with an aircraft that would be, due to its limited numbers, hard to maintain," Dow wrote. Two alternatives involved the purchase of American-built interceptors.

Diefenbaker knew that he would face serious political consequences for cancelling the Arrow program. A month after U.S. President Eisenhower and Secretary of State John Foster Dulles visited Ottawa and discussed general defence matters, Minister of Defence Pearkes went to Washington in August to discuss Canada's defence in general and the Arrow in particular with his U.S. counterpart, Neil McElroy. Reflecting the decisions made in the Pentagon in favour of electronic air defence systems, McElroy offered to share the cost of installing new radar, control systems and the Bomarc missile at Canadian military installations. McElroy told Pearkes the U.S. government would not buy any Arrows, and that should the Arrow be cancelled, U.S. interceptors would be available for sale to Canada at a lower price than the Arrows. "The August meeting between McElroy and Pearkes was the final straw that turned Diefenbaker's mind to cancellation," Dow wrote.

Other evidence also points to that month as the time when the Chiefs of Staff turned against the Arrow. In a memorandum dated August 25, 1958, which was unearthed in the 1990s by author Peter Zuuring, General Foulkes wrote: "I consider that the disadvantages far outweigh the advantages of continuing the CF-105 program. This conclusion has been reached after most thorough study of this problem by the Chiefs of Staff and myself." Foulkes warned that if the program continued, it would mean that Canada's defence budget would have to increase to "more than $2 billion for the next three to four years," this at a time when the federal government's total annual budget ran about $6 billion (compared to a 2006 budget of $180 billion).

Foulkes' memorandum came four days after the Cabinet Defence Committee met and endorsed the proposal to install two Bomarc missile bases in Eastern Canada, along with additional radars. The Bomarcs were designed to shoot down enemy aircraft but would not be useful against ICBMs. But they were "fully developed" at the cost of American taxpayers, the committee report said. The committee also recommended that "consideration be given to" ending the CF-105 Arrow program and considering replacements for the aircraft. The committee's report for Cabinet suggested that ICBMs would begin to decrease the threat of Soviet bombers in 1962 and 1963, and that with the use of Bomarc missiles, the RCAF would need only about 100 interceptor aircraft, a big drop from the 600 Arrows that had been forecast a few years previously. If the RCAF ordered only 100 Arrows, the cost per aircraft would come out to about $12.6 million, not counting the money spent already, and they would cost twice as much as 100 F-106 aircraft from the U.S. "Therefore the Chiefs of Staff consider that, to meet this modest requirement for interceptor aircraft, it would be more economical to procure a fully developed interceptor of comparable performance from United States sources," the committee report said.

Cabinet documents in the National Archives of Canada show that Pearkes himself had also decided that the Arrow program should end. The month of August had proven to be fateful for the Arrow, and so too would be the month of September, when Diefenbaker's Cabinet would grapple with the future of the Avro Arrow.

CHAPTER 23

The Government Acts

STARTING IN LATE AUGUST, a series of Cabinet meetings included discussions on the fate of the Arrow and were capped by an announcement from the prime minister. On August 28, the report of the Cabinet Defence Committee came before Cabinet, and Defence Minister Pearkes outlined its recommendations that the government accept the American offer of Bomarc missiles. Pearkes kicked off the discussions by saying the Arrow should be abandoned. If the RCAF equipped nine squadrons with 200 CF-105s, he said, the price tag would add up to $2 billion over four years. According to the Cabinet record "[Pearkes] himself recommended cancelling the CF-105 program in its entirety and deferring for a year any decision to order interceptor aircraft from the U.S.

"Not long ago, he had been disposed to recommend that it go ahead and aircraft be ordered for squadron service. However, the change in the nature of the threat and the great cost of development and production had brought him to make the recommendation he had," the Cabinet record said. Pearkes went on to say that the Bomarc "was cheaper than the CF-105 in terms of men and money, and just as effective." He also stated that the U.S. government would likely make nuclear warheads available for the Bomarcs; that the U.S. would not buy Avro Arrows, but could sell the F-106, which could be put into service faster than the Arrow at half the cost; and that the Americans were developing the F-108.

Pearkes' comments caused a "long discussion" in Cabinet, where it came out that the British government was not interested in buying the Arrow, and neither were other members of NATO. Although some Cabinet members said Canada's economy could withstand the blow of an Arrow shutdown, especially given its cost, others feared the economic consequences of cancelling the Arrow, which would cost 25,000 jobs at Avro Canada and its subcontractors, particularly at a time when the economy was slowing down. Cabinet discussed the strategic implications of the Arrow and of missiles. The discussion ended without a decision.

During that time, top officials from Avro had heard that their major project was in trouble, so they rushed to Ottawa to try to save it. With Crawford Gordon out of the country, Fred Smye and company director John Tory met with Diefenbaker, Pearkes and Finance Minister Donald Fleming. As Pearkes reported to Cabinet on September 3, just six days after their previous discussion of the Arrow, Smye and Tory "recommended that the airframe and Iroquois engine elements of the program be continued but that the fire-control system (Astra) and the weapon (Sparrow) projects be dropped and substitutes be obtained in the U.S." If 100 Arrows were ordered with Hughes MA-1 electronic systems and the Falcon missile, the cost per aircraft would fall to $8.9 million from $12.6 million.

Fleming recounted for Cabinet the arguments the two Avro officials had made about the impact cancelling the Arrow program would have on the economy. "Finally, they said that, if the program with their proposed modification were continued, their company would have a reasonable opportunity before the end of 1962 to look for other business," he said. "If they found little or none, then Avro would be in real difficulties."

The finance minister had told Tory and Smye that if the substitute fire-control system and missile were good enough for Canada, similar arguments could be made about the whole aircraft. Smye, Fleming said, was "very critical of some RCAF decisions and officers," a statement that caused Pearkes to speak in their defence. Pearkes also warned Cabinet that Avro savings estimates "should be treated with reserve."

Although they discussed the strategic threat that the Arrows would defend against and the consequences of cancelling the CF-105, Cabinet again deferred a decision on the matter and returned to the subject four days later.

That day's discussion was opened by Diefenbaker who, according to the meeting report, said the Cabinet ministers were close to agreeing that the military arguments weighed against the Arrow, but "the serious problem still requiring consideration was the effect on employment and the general economic situation."

Fleming recounted that one year previously, he had agreed to continue with the CF-105 because security was a top consideration, but now that the "military view was that the program should be cancelled, I did not see how the government could decide not to discontinue it." Although a cancellation would be difficult for the workers involved, Fleming said, they could be absorbed into the economy, which included an "important aircraft industry in Canada without the CF-105." He also argued for a cancellation sooner rather than later. "Finally, one had to keep in mind that by going ahead, and thereby adding approximately $400 million a year for four years to the defence appropriation, air defence would assume a disproportionate share in the defence budget. This was nearly the value of the year's wheat crop," he said, in an argument that must have impressed Cabinet ministers from the West, including the prime minister. "A good deal of northern development could be undertaken for much less. In short, cancelling the program would be of much greater help to the economy as a whole than continuing it," the finance minister concluded.

Although this meeting would not end with a decision, Cabinet ministers raised their concerns about cancelling the Arrow in the fall, when unemployment usually rose. They feared an immediate cancellation might "lead to a drastic downturn from which recovery would be extremely difficult." Cabinet's move on the Arrow was becoming more of a question of "when" rather than "if." Before Cabinet picked up the matter again, Avro Canada would make one more high-level appeal to the government.

On September 17, Crawford Gordon went to Ottawa and met with Pearkes, Fleming and then Diefenbaker. The meeting between Gordon and the prime minister has become one of the most controversial events in the history of Avro Canada. Gordon's biographer, Grieg Stewart, wrote that Gordon had arrived "bombed" from scotches he had consumed on the train to Ottawa, and then was forced to wait for his appointment with Diefenbaker, which made him angry. Stewart quoted John Pallett, the Member of Parliament for the constituency that included the Avro plant, who was waiting outside. Pallett said Gordon was "acting very childish," smoking a cigar in the presence of the non-smoking prime minister and shouting to the point where Diefenbaker considered having him ejected from the office.

In his memoirs, Diefenbaker wrote that Gordon began his presentation in a blustering fashion, banging his hand on the prime minister's desk for emphasis: "I stopped him immediately and pointed out that he was liable to do himself serious injury if he kept on banging his hand. That ended his bellicosity." Diefenbaker said Gordon warned that Avro Canada would be closed and thousands put out of work if the Arrow was cancelled.

"Mr. Gordon had recommended that production of the Arrow aircraft and the Iroquois engine be undertaken but the programs for the Astra fire-control equipment and the Sparrow missile be cancelled," Diefenbaker reported to Cabinet four days later. "There was nothing essentially new in his proposal."

Grattan O'Leary, a Conservative supporter and editor of the *Ottawa Journal,* was just outside the prime minister's office awaiting a meeting of his own when Diefenbaker received Gordon. "I was sitting in the anteroom when this fellow came out, and he was white as a sheet," O'Leary told journalist Peter Stursberg. "I was next in, and Dief said, 'I have just told him that the thing is off.' I said, 'Why did you tell him that?' He said, 'Look, this is going to cost a billion dollars. We have no market for them. So why do we spend a billion dollars on a plane that we have no use for? We don't need enough of them. We have no export market and no domestic market for these planes. They are costing too much and I had to tell him no.'"

Although Cabinet had not officially made its decision yet, most minds were already made up well before Gordon arrived in Ottawa. Regardless of Gordon's behaviour in the prime minister's office, the Avro president's chances of saving the Arrow were already very small. Four days later, Cabinet gathered again to decide the Arrow's fate.

Diefenbaker, Pearkes and Fleming reported on their meetings with Gordon, and the finance and defence ministers said Gordon's figures about possible savings from American-made Bomarc missiles and fire-control systems were not very precise and "appeared to be exaggerated." The Cabinet minutes stated that in the course of a long discussion, "few ministers had changed their minds on the desirability of cancelling the contracts for the Arrow and its associated equipment. The Cabinet was clearly divided in its view on the central question." They worried about continuing with the Arrow despite the fact that military opinion was moving against it.

As the discussion wound down, Diefenbaker presented a compromise "that might involve carrying on the development program until March but not beginning the production program on the Arrow or the Iroquois at this time. This continuation of development might be regarded as a form of insurance in the present tense situation." The compromise proposal won endorsement from Cabinet.

"If Diefenbaker had finally settled on a decision to cancel the Arrow, a flat announcement to that effect could have destroyed his government," James Dow wrote. "His instinct for political survival would have told him there was a need to prepare his ground." Two days later, the prime minister began to do just that.

Diefenbaker announced on September 23 in a five-page written statement that Cabinet had decided to build two Bomarc bases, one near North Bay, Ontario, and the second north of Ottawa in Québec. The Pinetree radar system would be strengthened and the semi-automatic ground environment (SAGE) control system would be installed to help direct the Bomarcs and interceptor aircraft towards any Soviet bombers.

Although this part of the decision had been relatively easy for Diefenbaker's Cabinet to make, its ramifications would later bring down his government.

Diefenbaker's statement announced that the Arrow would not be put into production, but that the development program would continue until March 31, 1959, at which time a review of the Arrow program would be concluded. Although work would continue on the Arrow aircraft and Iroquois engine, the government ended all work on the Astra weapons control system and the Sparrow missile. The Astra would be replaced by a Hughes Aircraft MA-1 weapons-control system and the Sparrow by a U.S. Falcon missile, both of which had already been developed. This decision would cut the price of each Arrow to $9 million from $12.5 million, Diefenbaker said, although Dow noted that the true cost per aircraft was actually lower in both cases.

"Although both the Arrow aircraft and the Iroquois engine appear now to be likely to be better than any alternatives expected to be ready by 1961, it is questionable whether, in any event, their margin of superiority is worth the very high cost of producing them by reason of the relatively small numbers likely to be required," the statement added.

"The Arrow supersonic plane has already thrilled us with its performance, its promise and its proof of ability in design and technology," Diefenbaker said. "However, it will be recognized, I believe, that as the age of missiles appears certain to lead to a major reduction in the need for fighter aircraft, Canada cannot expect to support a large industry developing and producing aircraft solely for diminishing Canadian defence requirements."

The prime minister prepared the ground to bring an end to the Arrow program with his statement, but different people would take their own meanings out of what he had said.

CHAPTER 24

On Life Support

THE NEXT DAY'S *Montreal Gazette* bore the headline: "Production of 'Arrow' Shelved, Switch to Missiles: Bomarc to Become Primary Weapon for Defence." Other press reports depicted the announcement as a death warrant for the Arrow, notably an article in October by veteran Ottawa correspondent and Arrow critic Blair Fraser in *Maclean's* magazine entitled, "What Led Canada to Junk the Arrow?" Fraser wrote, "The plain truth is, nobody thought the government would have the courage to make such a painful decision. The fact that the decision was right didn't carry enough weight. It meant an early end to more than twenty thousand jobs, most of them in the very heartland of the Conservative Party. It went against the emotional urges of all Canadian air force men, and of most air force veterans. It disappointed a big Canadian industry with many big Conservative shareholders. In short, it was political poison of a kind to scare any politician out of a year's growth."

"The uncertainty surrounding the future of the project and rumours of cancellation intensified after the September proclamation," Dow wrote. "No amount of effort could get a straight answer out of the government." Avro and Orenda noticed a new tone in all correspondence from the government, with wording designed to limit the government's liability for project costs.

At the time, Orenda was negotiating with the French air ministry and the Marcel Dassault Aircraft Company to equip France's Mirage IV fighter with Iroquois engines. According to Dow, Orenda managers were alarmed when French officials began to move away from the deal, which would have involved hundreds of engines and cost tens of millions of dollars, because the officials heard that the engine program would not be going on much longer.

The head of Orenda, Charles Grinyer, offered his resignation in the wake of Fraser's article in *Maclean's*. Fred Smye went to Washington to try to save the Arrow, and returned home with a letter from the Assistant Secretary of the Air Force that stated "the USAF would be quite happy to provide the fire control system, missile and other components free." When Smye took the letter to the Canadian government, he got no response.

Crawford Gordon also continued to fight for the Arrow. A few days after Diefenbaker's statement, Gordon sent a report to Avro Canada shareholders in which he stated his confidence that the Arrow and the Iroquois would move into production once the program had been reviewed.

When Avro held its annual shareholders meeting in late October, Gordon expanded on this theme, outlining three reasons why he believed the Arrow would go on. "For the foreseeable future, the manned interceptor will continue to be an essential part of the North American defence system. Pilotless interceptors, such as the Bomarc, complement it but cannot effectively replace it." To back up this argument, Gordon quoted Air Marshal C. Roy Slemon, the RCAF's former Chief of Staff who was then Deputy Commander-in-Chief of NORAD. Slemon warned that Canada must "maintain and improve our air defence system to cope with the manned bomber threat." Gordon also quoted James Douglas, Secretary of the U.S. Air Force, who spoke of new Soviet long-range bombers.

"Secondly, the Arrow was specifically designed to fit the RCAF requirement for a manned interceptor in the time period involved, and we believe that it still best fits that requirement," Gordon said. To back up his case, he quoted Diefenbaker's praise of the Arrow and spoke about the success of the Arrow's test flight program.

"Thirdly, the economies made possible by changing the fire-control system and armament, together with other economies which can be effected in the program, have reduced the unit cost of these aircraft to a point which we believe to be compatible with the Canadian economy," the Avro president said. He said the first 100 Arrows could be produced for $3.5 million each, rather than the $9 million figure used by Diefenbaker, which included the development and tooling costs that already had been spent.

Gordon raised Avro's important role in putting Canada at the "spearhead" of modern technology and international prestige. "Complete reliance on other countries for even the crucial weapons with which to defend ourselves would be a long step backwards from the position of independence which this country has been laboriously building over the years," Gordon said.

Avro management offered government officials including Pearkes the first 100 Arrows at a fixed price of roughly $3.5 million each and the next 100 at $2.6 million each, but they drew little interest from the government. With the prime minister spending much of the fall on a lengthy world tour, the government did little about the Arrow except to be on the receiving end of Avro's campaign to save the aircraft.

"In the months leading up to Christmas, A.V. Roe executives, led by Gordon, did just about everything they could to get into the press and extol the virtues of the Arrow and how vital it was to Canadian defence. No stone was unturned," wrote Greig Stewart. The efforts included an article in *Maclean's* by Gordon that refuted Blair Fraser's attacks on the Arrow, and press releases to Toronto papers discussing the company's importance to the local economy and tax base.

"The six months following the announcement regarding the Arrow put more pressure on Pearkes and caused him more sleepless nights than any other period in his career," wrote Pearkes' biographer, Reginald Roy. "Almost immediately, there was a flood of letters to him, to the prime minister and to members of Parliament from organizations and individuals expressing alarm at the possibility the Arrow might be scrapped."

Diefenbaker expressed his displeasure at Avro's campaign and at statements from Air Marshal Slemon, such as those quoted by Gordon. "Avro had put on a tremendous publicity campaign and this played right into their [the government's] hands," Diefenbaker said at the meeting. "If the government decided to continue development it would be accused of giving in to a powerful lobby. Pressure was coming in from other sources in Ontario, too." The campaign was not having its intended effect on the prime minister, though. Even if he thought the September decision was wrong, Diefenbaker told Cabinet he was determined to "adhere firmly to it" because of the pressure that had been brought to bear on the government.

At a pre-Christmas Cabinet meeting, Pearkes reported on a NATO meeting he attended in Paris in which he made one more pitch to the Americans to buy the Arrow. The U.S. officials were not interested and told him that they had "decided not to proceed with the development of any new interceptor aircraft except for the [F] 108, which was years in the future." According to Pearkes, this strengthened the government's resolve to abandon the CF-105.

~✖~

CHAPTER 25

Decision to Terminate

JANUARY 1, 1959, MEANT that the deadline facing the Avro Arrow was looming, and amongst those preparing for that decision was the Leader of the Opposition, Lester B. Pearson, who asked his now retired Liberal parliamentary colleague C.D. Howe for his opinion on the CF-105. "There is no doubt in my mind that the CF-105 should be terminated—costs are completely out of hand," Howe wrote on January 22, adding that he had been prepared to close down the program in 1957, once the election was over. Turning to Diefenbaker's September statement, Howe wrote, "subsequent expenditures on both aircraft and engine were definitely an unemployment relief measure, and an expensive one." Howe also provided advice on attacking the government once it had cancelled the Arrow, mainly by concentrating on the costs of delaying the cancellation.

The New Year also saw resumption of the Arrow discussion in Cabinet. Nine days earlier, Cabinet had briefly discussed the Arrow, with Pearkes reporting that the new electronics control system and missile in the Arrow meant that the aircraft could carry more fuel and could therefore fly for longer distances.

The new systems also meant that development of the Arrow could be sped up, with the first operational aircraft being ready by September 1960. Pearkes estimated that the costs per aircraft had dropped to $7.2 million per aircraft, still double Crawford Gordon's estimate.

Despite these positive developments, the defence minister remained against the Arrow. He also reported that the U.S. military had 800 interceptors on duty and funds for another 650. The U.S. had decided to cut short production of its own delta-winged fighter, the F-106 Delta Dart, and was moving the funds toward development of the F-108. "An additional 100 interceptors from Canada would make a small contribution," Pearkes said. "Furthermore, the CF-105 could not cover all of Canada. Its range was limited from 300 to 500 miles [500 to 800 kilometres]."

On January 28, Pearkes warned Cabinet that once the government's financial estimates for 1959–60 were tabled in the next few weeks, "it would become known that there was no provision for expenditure on the Arrow beyond April 1, except cancellation costs." The statement was further confirmation that the government had effectively sealed the Arrow's fate in September.

A week later, Pearkes formally recommended that the CF-105 program be terminated, and Diefenbaker called for a meeting of the Cabinet Defence Committee to ratify the recommendation. The recommendation came to Cabinet on February 10, and Pearkes added at that meeting that, though he believed the threat from Soviet bombers was diminishing, he could not promise that it would not be necessary to buy American interceptors if the Arrow was cancelled.

The Diefenbaker Cabinet made its final and formal decision on the Arrow on February 17. After the exhaustive discussion in previous meetings, which covered economic concerns, the fact that Canada would soon have to replace the F-86 aircraft it had on duty in Europe, and possible aircraft that could replace the Arrow, this meeting was anticlimactic. Cabinet minutes show that the entire Cabinet was in favour of cancellation. Diefenbaker began the discussion by saying that his announcement of the cancellation was being prepared for delivery three days later. After a short discussion, Cabinet ratified the prime minister's intentions by taking the formal decision to terminate the Arrow and the Iroquois. The Cabinet's decision also called for an exchange of notes with the U.S. government to implement agreements with them on the Bomarc missile and SAGE computer control system. The decision also noted, almost as an afterthought, that the government would announce "production sharing with the United States and the acquisition of atomic weapons" at the same time.

෴

CHAPTER 26

Final Tests

ALTHOUGH THE EXECUTIVES of Avro Canada were busy fighting off the threatened cancellation and looking with growing concern at the company's financial position resulting from the liabilities it had taken on for the Arrow and the Iroquois, testing of the Arrow and its engine gained momentum. On January 11, 1959, the fifth Arrow made its first flight, and the sixth Arrow, the first to be fitted with the Iroquois engine, took its place at the head of the CF-105 production line.

One Iroquois had already flown before preparations began to install the new engines on Arrow 6. In another example of American agencies cooperating with Canada in preparing the Arrow, the USAF had loaned Avro Canada a B-47 Stratojet, a six-engine bomber produced by Boeing. In addition to that, the USAF had trained three Orenda test pilots at McConnell Air Force Base in Wichita, Kansas. Orenda chief test pilot Mike Cooper-Slipper, pilot Len Hobbs and flight engineer Johnny McLaughlin had 10 weeks of training in the B-47 and were fully qualified to fly the aircraft at the end of their sojourn in Kansas. The B-47 loaned to Orenda was flown to Canadair in

Cartierville, Québec, for modifications that allowed the Iroquois to be attached to a pylon near the rear of the B-47, along with controls for the engine. The aircraft was also painted in RCAF colours.

Testing of the Iroquois on the B-47 was still going on in February 1959. Flying the B-47 with the powerful Iroquois engine attached proved to be a challenge, but the Orenda pilots ran the engine for 31 hours in the air. Once an Iroquois exploded during flight, and after a quick landing, Orenda found that a turbine blade had failed. The solution to the problem proved to include changes in the blade design. As part of Avro's public relations efforts, well-known journalist June Callwood flew on the B-47 to chronicle the work on the new engine.

Arrow 5's first flight caused its pilot, Spud Potocki, worry when an oil light went on in one of its two Pratt and Whitney J-75 engines. Potocki shut the affected engine down and returned to Malton on one engine. Avro mechanics were still trying to fix the problem in February, which was related to a broken seal in a gearbox.

Avro had considered exhibiting the Arrow at the Canadian National Exhibition air show in 1958, but caution ruled with the aircraft still in early testing, and so the Arrow did not appear at the event.

All of the Arrow flights began and ended at Malton until February 2, 1959, when Peter Cope was flying Arrow 4. During the flight, a Viscount landed at Malton and then became stuck at the junction of the airport's main runways. The remaining runway was considered too short for the CF-105, so Cope took the plane to RCAF Station Trenton. Cope's previous flight had involved the failure of his drag chute, so he was extra careful when he brought the Arrow down on the Trenton runway. The chute worked properly, and the landing was without incident. The next day, Potocki flew the Arrow back to Malton.

On February 19, Potocki flew Arrow 3 and made history when he took a second person on board, D.E. (Red) Darrah, who rode in the back seat to fine-tune the aircraft's fly-by-wire system. Darrah became the fifth person to fly on board the Arrow, and the only person to fly as a passenger. That afternoon, Potocki took Arrow 1 up for 50 minutes, flying at Mach 1.7.

While the flights continued, many people in the management suite anxiously awaited the news of what the government planned to do next with the Arrow. Just the day before Potocki made his two flights, John Plant, Avro's general manager, had warned a high official in the Department of Defence Production that the company had no plans for an orderly shutdown if the Arrow program were to be cancelled.

CHAPTER 27

Black Friday

FRIDAY, FEBRUARY 20, 1959, began as a normal winter workday for the engineers and workers at the Avro plant in Malton. Jim Floyd met that morning, as he did every day, with his top engineers to discuss production questions and technical issues with the Arrows under development. Mike Cooper-Slipper was preparing to take the B-47 into the skies for another test of the Iroquois engine. Fred Smye began a board meeting of the Avro subsidiary Canadian Applied Research. His boss, Crawford Gordon, was sleeping at the company estate after a late evening of trying to reach Cabinet ministers on the phone in another effort to save the Arrow.

With the two flights the previous day, the five Arrows had made a total of 66 flights, with 70 hours and 30 minutes in the air. Potocki had made 34 of those flights. The first Arrow had made 25 flights and the fifth Arrow only one. The sixth Arrow—the first to be fitted with the Iroquois engine—was just a few weeks away from its first flight. As on most other days at Avro, rumours flew that the Arrow would be cancelled, but by then, these rumours had become old hat. But that day, the rumours would become fact.

At 9:30 AM, Diefenbaker rose in the House of Commons to deliver what he called a "somewhat lengthy statement on the subject of one facet of the national defence of Canada."

"The announcement I wish to make has to do with the decision regarding our air defence, which was foreshadowed in the statement made by me to the press on September 23 last," Diefenbaker said. "The government has carefully examined and re-examined the probable need for the Arrow aircraft and Iroquois engine known as the CF-105, the development of which has been continued pending a final decision. The conclusion arrived at is that the development of the aircraft and Iroquois engine should be terminated now."

Like the September statement that "foreshadowed" that day's announcement, Diefenbaker's statement to the House of Commons was a carefully constructed brief for the prosecution of his policy. Despite its promise, the Arrow had been "overtaken by events" and by weapons such as the Bomarc. The prime minister raised other vague alternatives to the Arrow, and he discussed its limited range. When he turned to the cost of the CF-105, Diefenbaker used carefully selected figures to bolster his case that costs had soared out of control. He also avoided mentioning the costs of prolonging the program between September and February. He said "there is no other feasible or justifiable course open to us. We must not abdicate our responsibility to assure that the huge sums, which it is our duty to ask Parliament for defence, are being expended in the most effective way to achieve that purpose."

He then turned to the Bomarc missiles, SAGE control system and the new radar stations that he said would be jointly financed by the U.S. and Canadian governments, with the U.S. picking up two-thirds of the tab. Speaking of Bomarc, Diefenbaker said "the full potential of these defensive weapons is achieved only when they are armed with nuclear warheads." His government was involved in discussions with the U.S. government about this matter, and Diefenbaker expressed confidence that an agreement would be reached. Although it was barely noticed at the time, this part of his decision would return to haunt him and his government.

At the same time, Gordon Hunter from the Department of Defence Production called Smye out of his board meeting to tell him of the prime minister's announcement. At the Avro plant, Jan Zurakowski got the news from a newspaper reporter just as Diefenbaker was winding up his speech. Soon news reports of Diefenbaker's statements reached friends and relatives of Avro workers, and their telephone calls alerted workers inside the Malton plant.

Shortly after 11:00 AM, John Plant went to the public address system at Avro and told the workers of the prime minister's announcement: "We, the management of the company, had no official information prior to this announcement being made. The cancellation of the Arrow and the Iroquois have, however, been confirmed as fact by a Mr. C.A. Hore, the representative of the Department of Defence Production. It is impossible at this stage to give you any further

details, until such time as I receive the official tele-
gram from Ottawa. In the meantime, I would ask that
you continue with your work. Later on in the day, you
will be informed as to our future."

Soon telex messages arrived at the Avro and Orenda
plants from D.L. Thompson of the Department of
Defence Production. They read: "You shall cease all
work immediately, terminate subcontracts and orders,
place no further subcontracts or orders and instruct
all your subcontractors and suppliers to take similar
action."

Smye roused Gordon from his sleep with the bad
news, and they agreed to bring Avro's management
together, first at Briarcrest, then later at the company's
boardroom in the Malton plant. They decided that
there was no choice but to immediately halt all work
on the Arrow and the Iroquois and send the workers
home.

That afternoon, which came to be known as "Black
Friday," Gordon went to the public address system and
announced that the company had been ordered to
cease work on the aircraft and engine. "As a result,
notice of termination of employment is being given to
all employees of Avro Aircraft and Orenda Engines
pending a full assessment of the prime minister's
statement on our operation. We profoundly regret this
action but have no alternative since the company
received no prior notice of the decision, and therefore
we were unable to plan any orderly adjustment."

In one stroke, 14,528 employees of Avro Aircraft and Orenda engines were laid off. Inside the plant, a thunderous silence followed Gordon's stunning announcement. Then conversation picked up as the thousands of shocked Avro employees put down their tools, gathered their clothes and headed out. A huge traffic jam developed as everyone drove away into a February snowstorm. Those who showed up for the evening shift were turned away at the gate, and only security personnel remained. The afternoon news-papers appeared with screaming headlines about the demise of the Arrow.

When he got home, engineer George Watts was greeted with disbelief when he told his wife Norma that he'd been laid off. "She looked at me and she laughed. It wasn't until the next day that she finally realized I was telling her the truth, when I was look-ing through the paper for jobs."

"We went home, pulled everyone together and had a big party," Avro engineer John Hodge recalled. "We didn't know what to do or what was going to happen."

After all the rumours that hadn't proven true, many of the laid off employees could not believe that the Arrow was really finished. The March 31 dead-line for the Avro review was still weeks away, so Diefenbaker's announcement came as a surprise. Others wondered whether Avro's decision to lay off everyone on the spot was a huge bluff designed to force the government to reconsider. Those who weren't

mourning the events of the day spent the evening discussing their fates over the phone.

The hopes that the layoffs might be overturned
were reinforced over the weekend when some people were told to return to the plant on Monday to
clean up. Others found themselves being pulled
almost immediately to a new life outside Avro. Engineer George Harris was awoken by a telephone call
on Saturday morning, inviting him to breakfast at
the airport hotel. By noon, Harris had been hired by
North American Aviation in Columbus, Ohio, to work
on flight test instrumentation on the A-5 Vigilante
strike aircraft. He was one of the first of many Avro
engineers to find work in the U.S. aerospace industry.

❧❀❧

CHAPTER 28

The Reaction

FEBRUARY 23, 1959, MARKED the 50th anniversary of J.A.D. McCurdy's first powered aircraft flight in Canada with the *Silver Dart*. A special commemorative stamp was issued depicting the *Silver Dart* and three Arrows flying in formation. In Ottawa that day, the main topic of discussion was the Avro Arrow.

The media's reaction to the cancellation varied. In Toronto, the newspapers tended to be somewhat critical. Although the *Globe and Mail* accepted Diefenbaker's decision, it criticized the United States for not purchasing the aircraft. The *Toronto Star* called the decision "correct but badly fumbled." Newspapers in other parts of the country were more likely to accept the government's decision without reserve.

In the morning, Diefenbaker's Cabinet gathered to prepare for the debate they knew would come, given Avro Canada's reaction and the media coverage that followed.

"The two principal points of criticism on the decision to cancel the Arrow program were, first, that no efforts had been made to provide alternative employment for the Avro workers and, second, that Canada would be still further dominated by the United States." The Cabinet's suggested response to the first point was that the "company officers were well aware, or they should have been, that the contract might be cancelled and should have been making preparations accordingly." On the second point, the Cabinet discussion raised the point that "there would be other opportunities to assert Canadian sovereignty and independence," including "legislation to ensure the independence of Canadian companies."

That afternoon, George Pearkes kicked off debate in the House of Commons with a defence of the government's decision, noting the delays and increasing costs in the program, and the government's belief that "the threat of the manned bomber against this country is diminishing." Pearkes also discussed other expensive defence programs that the government would have to support, including new destroyer escorts and the CP-107 Argus maritime patrol aircraft.

Then it was the Opposition's turn to speak. The Liberals followed C.D. Howe's advice and did not directly attack the government's decision. Opposition Leader Pearson charged that the government "was guilty of fumbling, confusion and delay in its policies, and guilty of failure to plan ahead." Liberal member of Parliament Paul Hellyer, who in the future would create more than his share of controversy as defence minister, called on Diefenbaker to take action to "stop the exodus of Canada's future from this country."

Hazen Argue of the Co-operative Commonwealth Federation, forerunner to the New Democratic Party, asked about the fate of the newly unemployed Avro workers. "What happens to Canadian sovereignty in the very unbalanced partnership that the government has agreed to on behalf of this country?"

The top executives of Avro Canada held a press conference the same day at their headquarters on University Avenue in Toronto. Crawford Gordon said that so far only 12 people had been called back, and he spoke about his feelings for those who had lost their jobs. He said that he and Fred Smye would meet with the government to discuss six proposals to put people back to work, including continuing the Arrow; replacing the RCAF F-86 Sabres posted in Europe with Canadian-built aircraft; producing a jet transport; more development of the Avrocar, a vertical takeoff aircraft; and work in the nuclear power field or in building a satellite.

The next day, Gordon and Smye met a number of Cabinet ministers to put forward their proposals, but the meeting was inconclusive. Diefenbaker, who did not attend, told the media that his government's September decision was perceived by many people, but not Avro, as marking the end of the Arrow program. He also attacked the abrupt dismissal of workers despite his government setting aside $50 million to cover cancellation costs. "I say that its attitude in letting out thousands of workers, technical workers and employees on Friday was so cavalier, so unreasonable, that the only conclusion that a fair-minded person can come to is that it was done for the purpose of embar-rassing the government."

Also that day, thousands of Avro and Orenda work-ers took part in a rally at the CNE Coliseum in Toronto to demand financial compensation from the govern-ment and a callback to work. Ontario Premier Leslie Frost, who had complained "in pungent language" about the cancellation of the Arrow, tried to resusci-tate Avro Canada and, later, the Iroquois engine.

That week, about 1500 employees were called back to the plant at Malton to do maintenance work on CF-100s and their Orenda engines. A few worked on the Avrocar. Others were put to work arranging new jobs for some of their colleagues or drawing up ideas that might be used to save the company. By April 1, Avro and Orenda had recalled 2500 workers.

Avro management such as James Floyd, the firm's top engineer, tried to form teams of engineers that Avro could loan to firms and agencies for a few months until a new project could bring them back to Malton, but their efforts failed to bear fruit.

Although many people did get good offers of work elsewhere in Canada or in the U.S., these offers took time to materialize. Once the Avro employees absorbed the reality of the Arrow's cancellation, the need for new work became their major preoccupation. "Like everyone else, I had a mortgage, and I had just had another child," Bryan Erb recalled. "So you've got to figure out how to put bread on the table. After the first week or two, you realize it's not going to get turned around. Yes, there's severance benefits, but they would run out before too long."

George Watts remembered how he had voted for Diefenbaker's Conservatives to teach the arrogant Liberals a lesson: "We voted ourselves out of a job, out of a career or, in my case, out of the country. I haven't let my feelings influence my vote ever since. I think about it very carefully now."

Depending on their skills, experience and contacts, the Avro engineers dealt with many offers, or a lack of them. Many journeyed to various parts of the U.S. and Canada for job interviews. Some prospective employers set up shop in Toronto hotels, and many ex-Avro workers saw each other repeatedly as they went from one interview to another. Some weren't so lucky. "I put in 40 applications and never got an answer," Fred Matthews said of the early weeks after Black Friday. "Not only no acceptance, not even an answer. So things looked pretty bleak."

Many of the newly unemployed never got a good offer and left aviation for good. Because of the extremely high standards and high budgets of aircraft programs, some aeronautical engineers had trouble finding engineering jobs elsewhere because, as one of them put it, they "might just call for too much sophistication." A group of Avro engineers decided to leave engineering and go back to school to learn dentistry. Some of the British engineers considered going back to their home country, but most decided against returning to a country that was still emerging from postwar austerity and was still afflicted by open class divisions. Many, like George Harris, found work building missiles and aircraft in the United States. And a brand-new U.S. government agency, the National Aeronautics and Space Administration (NASA), hired some of Avro's top people to help them launch astronauts into space.

While the people who had built the Arrow looked for new challenges or just a new paycheque, questions remained over the fate of their handiwork. The government, for its part, had added up the cost of the program; at the end of the fiscal year in March, the government had spent $247 million for the aircraft and $132 million for the Iroquois engine, a total of $379 million.

CHAPTER 29

The Aircraft Destroyed

FOR ALL THE MONEY that had been spent on the Arrow, Canadian taxpayers had become the owners of five completed CF-105s and six others on the assembly line, with one near completion. The government also owned the manufacturing jigs and the plans that remained inside the plant at Malton.

On April 18, just short of two months after Black Friday, the *Globe and Mail* and other newspapers carried a story revealing that the Arrows were to be broken up for scrap. The issue was soon brought to the House of Commons in Ottawa. Destruction of the aircraft began and went on over the next few weeks. Despite efforts to block photographs of the destruction, a photographer, Herb Nott, rented a small aircraft and flew over the Avro plant in late May or early June, and his photos of the disassembled Arrows sitting on the tarmac appeared in the media soon after, once a government ban on the photos was lifted.

Avro workers carried out the initial destruction under orders from the government, and Fred Smye called his decision to carry out the government's order to destroy the aircraft the biggest mistake of his life. But the work was soon out of Avro's hands, because the Crown Assets Disposal Corporation contracted the remainder of the job and the disposal of the scrap metal to Lax Brothers of Hamilton, which won the tender for the job to dispose of the five completed aircraft, the six others on the assembly line and the jigs used to build the Arrows. They bid $304,000 for the remains of the Arrow. Sam Lax told Greig Stewart that the scrapping process took place under the close scrutiny of government inspectors. "We used saws— you couldn't use torches because it was too dangerous," Lax remembered. All the metal was taken by truck to the Lax Brothers' smelter.

Some parts, such as the Pratt and Whitney engines, were removed from the aircraft and returned to the United States. Most of the Iroquois engines were destroyed. The nose section and cockpit of the sixth Arrow was saved, however, and taken to the RCAF Institute of Aviation Medicine, where it remained until it was transferred to the National Aeronautical Collection in Ottawa, which today is located at the Canada Aviation Museum at the Rockcliffe Airport in Ottawa. There, the remaining Arrow nose section sits next to an Iroquois engine and the nose section of the Avro Jetliner.

Although many plans and documents were reportedly placed in secure storage, many parts and diagrams were preserved by workers at the Avro plant and have appeared in museums and other collections around the country.

The nose section of the sixth Arrow on display at the Canadian
Aviation Museum in Ottawa

~ఞC~

But the question remains—why were the Arrows
destroyed, and who ordered their destruction? Many
people believe that Diefenbaker ordered the destruction out of a vindictive streak or a desire to erase all
traces of what he had ended. But there is no hard evidence to support this allegation.

Documents declassified years after the demise of the
Arrow revealed that Defence Minister Pearkes, Air
Marshall Hugh Campbell and Minister of Defence Production Raymond Hurley, and officials of his department, were involved in the destruction of the Arrow.

A memorandum from Campbell to Pearkes describes
the five completed Arrows as "strictly development

prototypes" that had flown only a small fraction of the 1000 hours of flying time required to certify airworthiness. "Consequently, there is considerable development left to be done before they could be used by the RCAF. We have explored the possible use of these aircraft by the National Aeronautical Establishment (NAE) as research vehicles. However, since spare parts are in short supply, the aircraft would have to be maintained by Avro at Malton. Considering the development left to be done, the difficulties in supporting the aircraft and the cost of doing the research flying from Avro, it has been concluded that this approach is not practical. In summary, then, it can be said that there is no use in the RCAF or the NAE for these aircraft."

The memorandum also notes that the airframes on the unfinished aircraft and the Iroquois engines had not reached the point where they could be flown together, and the MA-1 fire-control system had not yet been installed on the Arrow. It then goes on to call for negotiations with the U.S. Air Force for return of the J-75 engines and the fire-control systems, and asks for Pearkes' permission to "make the necessary arrangements to dispose of the Arrow airframes and Iroquois engines," since "there is no particular use for the Arrow or its major components."

On April 8, Pearkes wrote back to Campbell stating that he understood there was no plan to fly or maintain the Arrows, and that efforts would be made to salvage parts that could be returned for credit. "The aircraft, as whole aircraft, will not be put up for disposal but will be reduced to scrap after all useful and creditable material has been removed." The defence minister then stated his agreement with the arrangements Campbell had proposed in his memorandum.

On April 24, Campbell wrote Pearkes to inform him that the scrapping of the five Arrows was being delayed "pending the outcome of the enquiries being made on behalf of the Royal Aeronautical Establishment, Farnborough, [England] of which I understand you are aware." Further letters, some dated as late as May 12, reference the delay in the destruction of the Arrows pending a decision from the British government.

A letter dating from 1960, from Minister of Defence Production Raymond O'Hurley stated "the RCAF asked the Royal Aeronautical Establishment if the aircraft would be useful in RAE's development programs and held up the order to destroy the aircraft while RAE considered the matter. Only after RAE indicated informally that no request would be made were the aircraft scrapped. This disposal order was given on May 15, 1959, three months after termination [of the Arrow program]."

O'Hurley's letter said that the British knew the Arrows were still in early phases of test flying and that "special arrangements for retention of tooling, personnel training, engineering support and a supply line of ground handling equipment and space would have had to be made at a prohibitive cost. It is my understanding that the United Kingdom's decision was based on the foregoing considerations; certainly it did not result from any influence exerted by the Canadian government."

His letter was written in reply to a query from a Conservative Member of Parliament who had read an article in the *Vancouver Province* written by the assistant publisher, A.R. Williams, who O'Hurley's letter identified as having once worked for Crawford Gordon at Avro. The article stated that the British government wanted to lease or buy three Arrows to run tests for a "super jet airliner" that would fly at supersonic speeds. "The Canadian government didn't actually refuse [the British request]. They thought about it for a while. They even held up for two weeks the order to destroy the planes. Then they asked the British to withdraw the request, which they did," Williams wrote. Similar versions of this story have appeared elsewhere, including in popular works about the Arrow. But none of the correspondence between the British and Canadian governments has ever turned up.

Another part of the controversy concerns the legend of "the Arrow that got away." Perhaps stirred in part by the salvage of the front end of the sixth Arrow, versions of this legend have one of the Arrows being flown away to a secret location, such as an isolated barn. Some people have reported hearing an Arrow in flight shortly after Black Friday. But no credible evidence has ever been advanced to suggest that an Arrow escaped the wreckers.

Finally, there remains the question of why the Arrows were destroyed. Although many have suggested political motives on the part of Diefenbaker and others, no evidence has been found to prove this idea. Nor has it been disproved. Dow wrote that all those who were or could have been involved in the decision to scrap the Arrow "contend that once the decision was made to cancel, all else was a follow-through based on standard operating procedures and was therefore the concern of lower echelons in National Defence and Defence Production." The Arrow involved highly classified technology, and part of the motivation for its destruction may have been to avoid security problems. Or, it may have simply been an overzealous effort to earn back money from the scrap metal.

In the 1950s, there were very few air museums compared to the present day, and no known offers were made at the time to preserve an Arrow in a museum or aircraft collection. In the 1940s and 1950s, thousands of aircraft that had flown in World War II were being reduced to scrap. Today, there are very few operating examples of many World War II aircraft. Although newspapers warned that the Arrows were about to be scrapped, no one launched a formal protest or organized a demonstration. But as time went by, growing numbers of Canadians saw the destruction of the Arrows as an act of vandalism of the worst order.

CHAPTER 30

The Avrocar

AFTER THE DEMISE of the Arrow, Avro Canada had one more aircraft program in development, one that has also become the stuff of legend. The Avrocar, Canada's own flying saucer, was Avro Canada's contribution to the raft of unusual aircraft designed in the early years after World War II. The war brought many companies and individuals into the field of aeronautics, resulting in the development of new engines, especially jet engines, and new frontiers in aircraft, notably in supersonics, which led to the creation of new types of aircraft. Two of the most famous were the U.S.'s Northrop Flying Wing and the Chance-Vought Flying Pancake.

Another popular area for investigation was in aircraft known as Vertical Takeoff and Landing (VTOL). These aircraft were developed with the hope of dispensing with airports, allowing aircraft to land where they were needed. Experimental VTOL aircraft of this era included aircraft that stood on end, such as the Ryan X-13 Vertijet; craft that relied on the brute force of their engines, such as the Rolls-Royce Flying Bedstead; aircraft with tilting wings; and crosses between winged craft and helicopters. Probably the most

The Avrocar

~✖~

famous VTOL aircraft is the Harrier Jump Jet combat aircraft.

At Avro Canada, John Frost had formed a Special Projects Group in 1951 after he left the CF-100 program while the company dealt with the aircraft's wing spar problem. Frost was an Englishman who worked at de Havilland Aircraft in the UK. He became known for his innovative ideas in aircraft design, including contributions to the Vampire fighter and then as project engineer on the DH-108 Swallow, the experimental swept-winged aircraft that test pilot Geoffrey de Havilland Jr. flew in 1946 when he died trying to be the first break the sound barrier. The Swallow later set speed records and became the first jet aircraft to break the speed of sound (the Americans had first broken the sound barrier in rocket-propelled craft).

In 1947, Frost joined Avro Canada, and while he worked on the CF-100, he also continued to think about new ideas for aircraft, an interest he was free to indulge when Avro agreed to his Special Projects Group. Bill Zuk, in his book about the Avrocar, wrote that Frost was interested in the reports of flying saucers that proliferated in the late 1940s and also followed reports of the various exotic aircraft being tested at the time. Frost was also looking at the ground cushion concept, as were researchers in other countries. (Christopher Cockerell, whose work in England led, in 1959, to the world's first hovercraft, which flies just above the ground or water on a thin cushion of air.) Frost began experimenting with small, disc-shaped models and was also thinking about new types of engines that might allow such a vehicle to fly.

Frost began thinking about a supersonic aircraft that would be controlled by altering the direction of thrust forces and that had an engine rotor that also served as a gyroscope to stabilize the aircraft. In 1952, along with Waclaw Czerwinski, Frost came up with a spade-shaped "all-wing supersonic aircraft" known as Project Y, which would take off vertically. Avro agreed to fund work on the project, and Frost and his team began building mock-ups.

In 1953, when Project Y gained some media publicity despite efforts to keep it secret, it drew criticism from C.D. Howe and from other Avro engineers who wanted resources focused on the CF-100. But that fall, a team of American experts headed by Lieutenant General Donald L. Putt, head of the USAF's research and development command, came to Avro to see the CF-100 and also got a briefing on Project Y. Frost's team was moving on to a new saucer-shaped design known as Project Y2, and in 1955, the USAF issued a contract to Avro Canada for continued work on Project Y2, which picked up on work supported by Avro and a reluctant Canadian government.

In 1957, a U.S. Army delegation led by its research and development chief, Lieutenant General Arthur G. Trudeau, came to Avro for a briefing on the work the company was carrying out for the USAF. "The army required a tactical craft that would give soldiers in the field greater mobility and was interested in vehicles that could hug the ground—Project Y2 could in ground-cushion mode," Zuk wrote. The army had provided financial support to various contractors for such things as rocket packs and flying platforms, but none had proven satisfactory.

The next year, the U.S. Air Force and Army signed an agreement with Avro to build the Avrocar, a saucer-shaped vehicle powered by three turbojet engines that turned a central turbo-rotor to generate downward thrust. Separate cockpits were built for a pilot and observer. This craft was much closer to what the army wanted than what the air force wanted, but it was seen as an important development step on the way to the supersonic aircraft, and Frost's team continued to work on both ideas. The cancellation of the CF-105 Arrow and the resulting layoffs also affected Frost's team. Although everyone outside the executive suite at Avro was sent home on Black Friday, engineers, some from outside the Special Projects Group, were rehired in March.

In April 1959, the existence of the Avrocar was publicly announced, and the following month, the first Avrocar was completed. The Avrocar was tested in a special rig at Malton, which revealed problems with the central rotor and noise and heat from the engines. The vehicle was shipped to the NASA Ames Research Center in California for wind tunnel testing, which began in 1960.

The second Avrocar was completed in August 1959 and made its first flight on September 29 with Avro test pilot Spud Potocki at the controls. The Avrocar was tethered to the ground for its first flights, and free flights began in December. Potocki and U.S. test pilots found that the vehicle could not rise much more than a metre off the ground. "Its ability to rise, hover and fly at top speed was extremely disappointing," Zuk wrote. But the Avrocar's worst problem was maintaining control. The Avrocar didn't have the tail, rudder or stabilizers of regular aircraft, and Frost's idea of closing and opening vanes to direct thrust from the engine didn't work.

The Americans spent $7.5 million on the Avrocar and associated research, but the Avrocar and the Special Projects Group's research on advanced supersonic

aircraft wound down in 1961 when the American contract wasn't renewed. American military leaders had
concluded that too much development work would be
needed before a vehicle such as the Avrocar would
prove useful.

The Avrocar has gone down in the history of flight
as the first major effort to build a flying saucer, and
the hope the U.S. military briefly invested in the Avrocar remained in the form of fanciful artists' concep-
tions of the Avrocar being used in combat and of more
advanced saucer vehicles in flight. Avro hoped to
develop the Avrocar into a larger combat vehicle and
even into a civilian Avromobile that would replace
automobiles, moving on a cushion of air rather than
on tires.

Since the two Avrocars were the property of the
U.S. military and bore both U.S. Army and Air Force
markings, they now reside in the U.S. The first Avro-
car was donated to the National Air and Space
Museum following its testing at the Ames Research
Center and is now in storage in a warehouse in Mary-
land. The second Avrocar is on outdoor display at the
U.S. Army Transportation Museum at Fort Eustis,
Virginia.

When the Avrocar program came to an end in 1961,
it marked the end of Avro Canada's final aviation
effort. Many people believed that the Avrocar concept
was deeply flawed, while others maintain that it was
too far ahead of its time. In designing the Avrocar,
Frost had hoped to build a supersonic vehicle that even

now, 50 years later, still resides in the realm of the imagination. But he got caught in the realities of building a less ambitious aircraft that relied on the ground effects that are today used in hovercraft. "The irony was that at Malton, Mr. Frost's eyes had been so set on the skies he failed to spot the Avrocar's ground-hugging potential under his nose," British journalist Julian Borger wrote. With the Avrocar's association with flying saucers, this most modest of Avro projects remains almost as memorable as the Arrow.

CHAPTER 31

Avro Dreams Dashed

JOHN FROST AND HIS Special Projects Group weren't alone at Avro Canada in looking beyond the Arrow. Many people at Avro realized that the company would need more than one major project at a time if it were to survive and prosper. As James Floyd put it, "the fact that there was only the Arrow worried me sick." Jim Chamberlin, the Arrow's chief aerodynamicist, led engineers who examined improved versions of the Arrow and similar aircraft, such as supersonic transport aircraft. Under the direction of Mario Pesando, another research team of engineers also took initial stabs at various projects such as missiles, a supersonic transport aircraft, a satellite launch capability for the Arrow, and even a "space threshold vehicle."

Naturally, derivatives of the Arrow drew a great deal of attention. The five Arrows that flew with the J-75 engines were known as Mark I Arrows, and the sixth Arrow that headed up the assembly line on Black Friday was to be equipped with Iroquois engines and would therefore have been the first Mark 2 Arrow. Because the Iroquois engine was both lighter and more powerful than the J-75 engine, the Mark 2 Arrows were expected to be able to fly faster than Mach 2 and remain in the air longer than the Mark 1 Arrows. Avro was drawing up plans for improved Mark 2 Arrows that could fly longer distances, and was studying a Mark 3 Arrow that could fly up to Mach 2.5 and for even longer distances. These CF-105s would have looked almost the same as the earlier versions, but they would have been equipped with variable intakes for the jet engines in place of the fixed intakes on the Mark 1 and 2 Arrows. The engine nozzles would also have been different, and other minor changes would have been needed to deal with the increased heat loads on the aircraft surfaces.

Avro was also working on a reconnaissance version of the Arrow, a training version, and even a bomber version that might have interested the Royal Air Force in Britain. Another concept had the Arrow launching missiles that could attack ICBMs or carrying satellites into orbit. Many of these ideas were feasible because of the flexibility built into the Arrow with its weapons pack, which could be easily changed out for different purposes depending on the mission.

And inevitably, Avro engineers were also sketching out ideas for an Arrow 4, capable speeds of Mach 3 or better, with an even longer mission radius than previous versions of the Arrow. As James Floyd said, "the Arrow Mark 1 that flew in 1958–59 was only the first of a fine family of aircraft. With normal development, it would have been a most interesting family."

While *Sputnik* signalled the arrival of missile-based warfare, it more famously marked the beginning of the space age, and so, in the late 1950s, almost every company involved in building advanced aircraft was looking at building spacecraft that could be used for peaceful exploration of space or on this new military frontier. In 1958, engineers at Malton were designing a winged Space Threshold Vehicle. This vehicle drew from ideas developed in Germany in the period prior to World War II, when designers such as the Austrian Eugen Sänger and his wife Irene Bredt drew up designs for a winged craft that could go into orbit and back. In the late 1950s, the Soviet space program and the U.S. Air Force were looking at developing such craft. But the difficulties of building such vehicles and the growing ability to carry out military work in space without astronauts postponed the era of winged spacecraft until the launch of the first space shuttle in 1981.

Pesando's group and another team headed by Rolf Marshall examined other future projects for Avro, including nuclear research, missiles, gyrocopters, new forms of propulsion, new materials, monorail and other transit projects, and general systems work.

Although Avro was beginning to look forward to the day it could diversify, the fact remained that it had placed a dangerous level of reliance on one product, the CF-105 Arrow, and one customer, the Canadian government. The paper dreams of Avro Canada also existed on many drawing boards in the U.S. and western Europe, but the question remains of how Canadian technology would have evolved had Avro Canada remained in operation.

Some of the Avro concepts have never come to fruition. And many of the ideas being developed at Avro
were beyond the means of Canadian taxpayers, just as
Diefenbaker and his colleagues suggested was the case
for the Arrow. And though some of Avro's ideas might
have become reality, it is also possible that the cost of
realizing these dreams might have dashed other
dreams that *did* come true in the Canada of the late
20th century.

～❀～

CHAPTER 32

Avro's End

IN THE SPRING OF 1959, Canada's third largest corporation was in deep, deep trouble. It had become dependent on one product and one customer, and that customer had rejected the product. Although some workers and engineers had been called back to do maintenance work on CF-100s and continue development of the Avrocar, most of the company's best talent was on the unemployment line or already at work elsewhere. And despite Avro's hopes of developing new aircraft, hopes that were frequently invoked after Black Friday, there was no clear plan to save the company.

On April 8, Walter MacLaughlin resigned as executive vice-president of Orenda Engines, and he was soon followed by several of the top executives at Avro and Orenda. Many others resigned in the weeks that followed, or like James Floyd, were lured back to England to work on other aircraft.

As for Crawford Gordon, he disappeared from the Avro offices and was reputed to have resigned on Black Friday. He hadn't resigned, but he did little work and sought solace in drinking. Finally on June 17, Sir Roy Dobson wrote Diefenbaker with an announcement. "I have asked for and received the resignation of Mr. Crawford Gordon as President of A.V. Roe Canada Limited on the grounds that I was most dissatisfied with his work and his actions, which have not been in the best interests of the company or the country." On that occasion, Gordon and Dobson spoke of their regard for each other, but Dobson was bitterly disappointed in the younger man. He had come to see Gordon as a friend who had presided over the loss of the Arrow and descended into personal problems that included the dissolution of his marriage and excessive drinking. On June 30, the 44-year-old Gordon left his office on University Avenue for the last time. Dobson soon appointed Harvey Smith to take over the company, and Smith began by firing John Plant and Fred Smye.

Avro struggled on with the Avrocar and other projects such as building boats and even manufacturing pots and pans. Smith and his successor, Ted Emmert, tried to develop new aircraft programs or ventures in other forms of transportation, but to no avail. On April 30, 1962, A.V. Roe Canada and the Avro name passed into history when the company changed its name to Hawker Siddeley Canada at a meeting presided over by Dobson, the man who had started it all.

That year, the Avro plant at Malton was sold to de Havilland Aircraft. It was soon put into use for the fabrication of wings and tail assemblies for Douglas DC-9 aircraft, and later, under the control of McDonnell Douglas Canada, wings for the DC-10 and parts for other McDonnell Douglas Aircraft. When McDonnell Douglas was absorbed by Boeing in 1997, the plant became Boeing Toronto, and wings for Boeing 717 were manufactured there, along with parts for the Delta rocket, the C-17 Airlifter and the 737 Jetliner. The old Avro sections of the plant were demolished in 2003, and Boeing shut down the operation in 2005.

Hawker Siddeley Canada carried on with the remaining assets of the company and concentrated on making railcars and subway cars before these operations were sold to other companies such as SNC-Lavalin and Bombardier, and the company was ultimately dissolved. Another property held by the company from Crawford Gordon's acquisition binge was Dominion Steel and Coal Corporation, based in Nova Scotia. In the early 1960s, Dosco closed down its mines and other money-losing operations under pressure from Hawker Siddeley management. When Dosco announced in 1965 that its mines were nearing the ends of their productive lives, and that they faced closure in the near future, the federal government stepped in and created the Cape Breton Development Corporation, which expropriated Dosco's mines and oversaw their phasing out through the remainder of the 1960s and into the 1980s. Other coal mines opened by the development corporation carried on until 2001.

In 1967, the Nova Scotia government took over the Sydney Steel Mill that had belonged to Dosco, planning to sell it back to private owners within a year. Instead, the government continued to operate the steel mill until 2001. Both provincial and federal governments provided heavy subsidies to keep the mines and the mill going. Even after these operations closed, governments faced heavy costs for environmental cleanup, especially of the infamous tar ponds left behind from the coke ovens that provided fuel for the steel mill. It would be interesting to speculate on how the Nova Scotia operation would have fared had Avro Canada continued as a major aircraft manufacturer, and how much money governments would have saved had they not felt obliged to keep the mines and the mill operating at taxpayers' expense.

~⋇~

CHAPTER 33

End of the Iroquois

THE OTHER MAJOR PIECE of Avro Canada that continued to operate was Orenda Engines, and this story is a happier one than Dosco and its successors. The Orenda engine that the firm had built for the CF-100 had been a success, and it was also manufactured for use in the Canadian-built F-86 Sabres. The success with the CF-100 and the Orenda engine led Avro to try and repeat the feat with the CF-105 and the Iroquois, a decision that contributed to the pressures that led to the demise of both the aircraft and engine.

While the Iroquois was in production, Orenda Engines executives such as Charles Grinyer were looking to markets beyond the Arrow. Orenda hoped to sell the engine to equip Mirage IV aircraft built by Marcel Dassault in France, but the French backed off when the Canadian government began to pull away from the Arrow in September 1958. Grinyer entered into an arrangement with Curtiss-Wright in the United States to manufacture the Iroquois under licence. Harry Keast, an Orenda engineer, told Greig Stewart that the American firm was moving out of the jet engine field: "They were restricted to building rockets, and what's more, they were just about the worst company we could have chosen to pick up the option because it blocked us from offering it to anybody else."

Dassault looked again at the Iroquois after Black Friday, but according to James Dow, nothing happened. "If the federal government had been prepared to write off development costs of about $100 million, costs that would be lost in any event by termination, then the Iroquois would certainly be a marketable item," he wrote.

There is also the question of how much development work remained to be done on the Iroquois engine, and what the remaining development costs would have been. Years after the program was cancelled, Charles Grinyer, whose pioneering work made the Iroquois arguably the most advanced part of the whole Arrow package, discussed in an interview with Peter Zuuring the many materials and design advances that went into the engine, including new fabrication and welding techniques and the use of new materials such as plastics. Although the engine was undergoing flight testing on the B-47 and was to be installed on the next Arrow on the assembly line, it was still some distance from being a perfected item in full production. Grinyer told Zuuring that turbine blades were failing because of vibration problems, which were being researched when the program was cancelled. So putting the engine into production would have been challenging. The Iroquois engine was made of exotic elements, especially titanium, which is difficult to mould or machine into parts, and these were huge challenges in 1959. Although Orenda was making progress with the engine at the time of Black Friday, Grinyer estimated that it needed another year of work to overcome its problems.

To bring the Iroquois into full production would have required more money for research and development, and Avro's main source of funding stopped on February 20, 1959. The government's decision to halt the Iroquois along with the Arrow can be questioned, as can Avro Canada's decision not to carry on with the Iroquois using its own funds.

The end of the Arrow meant the end of Avro Canada, but the end of the Iroquois did not mean the end of Orenda Engines. In the summer of 1959, the Canadian government decided to use Lockheed F-104 Starfighters for the RCAF in Europe, and the government and contractors agreed that the aircraft would use General Electric J-79 engines built under licence by Orenda engines. Similar contracts followed, including building the engines for the CL-41 Tutor trainer, which still serves as the aircraft for the Snowbirds Demonstration Team, and the Canadian version of the F-5 fighter.

Orenda Engines became part of the Magellan Aerospace Corporation in the 1980s, and as part of Magellan, it still produces aircraft engines and does engine maintenance and repair work, as well as producing components for other engine manufacturers. Today it remains the only surviving element of Avro Canada.

CHAPTER 34

New Aircraft

THE CANADIAN GOVERNMENT didn't have to wait long after Black Friday to face another decision about acquiring aircraft for the RCAF, this time for use in Europe. The Air Division in Europe had been equipped with Canadian-made F-86 Sabres, and then with CF-100s. Although some people had expressed a hope that the Arrow might be deployed in Europe, changes in American military doctrine toward massive retaliation in a full-out nuclear war meant a change for the RCAF in Europe from a defensive role where the Arrow might have been useful. "Canada was asked to switch its air force in Europe to a strike-reconnaissance role in which Canadian pilots would carry American nuclear warheads against targets inside the Soviet Union," Dow wrote. And the Arrow wasn't suitable for this new role.

The Canadian government received a number of proposals for the new aircraft to go with the RCAF's new role in Europe. One proposition from Republic Aviation in the U.S. involved building the F-105 Thunderchief for the RCAF at Avro Canada under licence. But the government opted instead for Lockheed's F-104 Starfighter, which was built under licence at Canadair in Montréal. The one bright spot for Avro was that the engine contract for the aircraft was awarded to Orenda engines.

Although the government's decision did not address the issue of other aircraft to replace the Arrow, that role being left to the Bomarc missile, the RCAF began lobbying for another aircraft, arguing that bombers still posed a threat to Canada and the United States. The Diefenbaker Cabinet began considering the matter in 1960, though Cabinet minutes at the time recorded concern about the damage that statements made at the time of the Arrow cancellation had done to the government's position: "To obtain other aircraft now, in the face of statements that threat of the manned bomber was diminishing and that the day of the interceptor would soon be over, would be most embarrassing."

The matter soon became the subject of negotiations between the U.S. and Canadian governments, and though Canada rejected the idea of receiving McDonnell F-101 Voodoos from the U.S. as a gift, Canada acquired 66 used Voodoos as part of a complicated agreement reached in June 1961 that also involved work on NORAD radar sites in Canada and manufacturing incentives for armament production. The aircraft were turned over to Canada starting the following month and throughout the fall. New F-101s were acquired in the early 1970s and remained in Canadian service until 1984. The Voodoos were criticized for their relative lack of power compared to the Arrow and because they were second-hand, an issue that became more critical as the aircraft grew older. But the Voodoo turned out to be dependable and ultimately carried out its assigned role successfully. For two decades, the aircraft was used to intercept and escort off-course airliners and the occasional Soviet Tu-95 Bear bomber flying to Cuba or testing North American air defences.

In the late 1960s, the Canadian Forces supplemented its Voodoos and Starfighters with the F-5 Freedom Fighter, a lightweight, low-cost fighter developed by Northrop, which remains in service in many places around the world. The Canadian version, known as the CF-5, was built under licence at Canadair and supplied with General Electric J-85 engines built by Orenda. The CF-5 was built in both one-seat and two-seat versions and was used by two Canadian squadrons that could be deployed quickly. Some of the CF-5s were not used in Canada and instead were sold to Venezuela.

In the late 1970s, the Canadian Forces launched a competition for a new generation of fighter aircraft. Although many experts called for two different planes, one to cover Canada's European role with NATO and another to guard Canada against Soviet bombers, the government decided to choose one aircraft to equip Canadian fighter pilots in both Canada and Europe. And so the contract promised to be the most expensive arms procurement in Canadian history to that time. The aircraft in contention included the Northrop F-18L, the Grumman F-16 and F-14, the McDonnell Douglas F-18A Hornet and F-15, and the European

Tornado fighter. In 1980, the Canadian government chose the McDonnell Douglas F-18A Hornet, which went into service as the CF-18. The single-seat fighter was originally developed for the U.S. Navy, and Canada was the aircraft's first non-American customer. Canada bought 138 CF-18s, and unlike the CF-104s and CF-5s, the aircraft were made in the U.S., albeit with Canadian subcontracting work. Most of the CF-18s are single-seaters, but some are equipped with two seats for training.

The CF-18 has been upgraded and will remain in use as Canada's primary fighter aircraft for a number of years. Unlike previous Canadian jet fighters, the CF-18 has been used in combat, first as Canada's contribution to the Gulf War in 1991 to liberate Kuwait from Iraqi forces and then as a fighter and bomber when NATO forces intervened in the former Yugoslavia in 1999.

The Voodoo and its successors formed only one part of the replacement force for the Arrow. Although these aircraft have been relatively uncontroversial, the armament they used in the 1960s and 1970s was a point of contention. The other part of the Arrow's replacement was a missile whose name, like that of the Arrow, instantly evokes controversy.

CHAPTER 35

The Bomarc Missile

WHEN JOHN DIEFENBAKER heralded the demise of the Avro Arrow in 1958, he announced that Canada would procure Bomarc surface-to-air missiles. The announcement was couched in rhetoric about Canada entering the missile age and the promise that the missile could be used with either conventional or nuclear weapons. Five months later, when Diefenbaker announced the end of the Arrow program, the Bomarc again figured prominently in his announcement. This time, the prime minister announced that the Bomarcs would be equipped with nuclear warheads, and at the same time he stated that Canada's army and navy would also be equipped with nuclear arms.

The announcements of the Bomarc and of nuclear arms took second place on both occasions to what Diefenbaker had to say about the Arrow, and today those decisions are largely forgotten while debate still continues over the CF-105. Yet the armament decisions led to a great controversy in the early 1960s that played a major role in Diefenbaker's fall from power four years after his government cancelled the Arrow.

In 1958, Defence Minister George Pearkes and his military chiefs looked at a whole set of different air

Bomarc-B missile

defence options for Canada, including missiles such as
the Nike Hercules and the Bomarc. They opted for the
Bomarc, which had a far greater range and was projected to cost less than the Nike Hercules. The decision
for the Bomarc was duly announced, but as study
work on the weapon went on that fall, a new version
of the missile, the Bomarc-B, which was still being
developed, came under consideration. Unlike the earlier version, the Bomarc-B depended on the Semi-
Automatic Ground Environment (SAGE) computer
detection and control system being developed in the
U.S. And the Bomarc-B was designed to use only
nuclear warheads. Hence, when Diefenbaker cancelled the Arrow, he announced that the Bomarc-B
would be used and therefore committed Canada, at
least on paper, to nuclear weapons.

The Bomarc got its name from the Boeing Company, which developed the missile along with the
Michigan Aerospace Research Center (MARC). Standing 14 metres high, the Bomarc used two ramjet
engines to propel it at nearly three times the speed of
sound, after an initial boost at launch from a solid-
fuelled rocket. The Bomarc could cruise at a high of
21 kilometres for a distance of up to 600 kilometres
from its launching site, and its 10-kiloton nuclear warhead was designed to explode when the missile came
close to its target (having it strike its target would have
been a major technical challenge in the 1950s and
1960s). Because the missile could only get close to its
target, it required more powerful nuclear warheads

whose explosions were more likely than conventional warheads to knock the target out of the sky.

The Bomarc was the largest surface-to-air missile built to that time, and it was the only missile of its type ever deployed by the U.S. Air Force. All other missiles of this type were built and deployed by the U.S. Army. The Bomarc, with its ramjet engines and air force heritage, was sometimes considered a pilotless aircraft, and in its later years, the USAF used Bomarcs as target drones. The first Bomarcs began flying in 1952.

Although the Canadian government briefly considered basing Bomarcs elsewhere in Canada, the RCAF set up two squadrons equipped to launch Bomarcs, one near North Bay, Ontario, and the second near La Macaza, Québec, protecting Canada's major eastern population centres. Each squadron was equipped with 28 Bomarcs that were stored in "coffins," large sheds with hydraulically moveable roofs. When the missiles were put on alert, they were stood up to their launch positions.

The Diefenbaker government's Bomarc decision drew some negative comments at the time that were drowned out by the publicity over the demise of the Arrow. The criticism increased when testing of the Bomarc-Bs in the United States did not go well in 1959 and 1960. Its first six launches failed, and other tests were postponed. Debates about the proper tools for air defence that surrounded the Arrow and the Bomarc in Canada also roiled in the United States, and some of this discussion included questions about the utility of the Bomarc, even as the first USAF Bomarcs were placed on operational status in the U.S. in 1959.

The same strategic calculations of the Soviet shift from bombers to ICBMs that led to the Arrow's cancellation also caused the USAF Chief of Staff to recommend that most funds be cut from Bomarc-B development. In April 1960, the U.S. House of Representatives voted to cut off Bomarc funding, but the U.S. Senate saved the missile. The two bodies haggled over the Bomarc's fate and cut back the number of sites planned for the U.S. from 18 to 7. Work on building the two Canadian sites continued. Timely successes of Bomarc launches that spring also helped save the program. These controversies did not go unnoticed north of the border, and the Bomarcs became part of the controversy that swirled in Canada about the nation's increasing dependence on the U.S. military and U.S. defence industry.

The situation became even more complicated in 1960, when personalities changed on both sides of the border. In June, Diefenbaker appointed a new external affairs minister, Howard Green. An old friend of the prime minister, the British Columbian had not been overseas since his service in World War I. Green had strong views in favour of nuclear disarmament that were called a "magnificent obsession." He and his deputy minister, Gordon Robertson, worked against Canada taking up nuclear arms.

Pearkes had a different view, but his advancing age and the stress resulting from his decisions on NORAD, the Arrow and the Bomarc caused him to look to retire from active politics, and that October he left Ottawa to return to B.C. as lieutenant-governor. His replacement as defence minister, a Calgary MP named Douglas Harkness, had strong views in favour of arming Canada's forces with nuclear weapons, but Harkness did not have the friendship or influence with Diefenbaker that Pearkes did.

Three weeks after Pearkes left Cabinet, U.S. voters narrowly elected a young Democratic senator from Massachusetts, John F. Kennedy, to replace Eisenhower in the White House. Diefenbaker had strong anti-American and pro-British and pro-Canadian biases, but his similar background and age to Eisenhower and his admiration for Eisenhower's exploits directing European forces in World War II had helped ensure a smooth relationship between the two men.

Kennedy's youth, patrician airs and intellectual inclinations put off the Canadian prime minister, and the American president, who did not trust or understand Diefenbaker, quickly repaid the dislike. Kennedy took office early in 1961, and a month later, the two leaders held their first meeting in Washington, followed by Kennedy's visit to Ottawa in May.

The Kennedy administration's new "flexible response" doctrine looked at new ways to deploy limited nuclear weapons as a means of dissuasion short of all-out nuclear war. Diefenbaker had never been strongly interested in military matters, and when he had signed onto NORAD and NATO, commitments that implied the use of nuclear weapons, many observers questioned whether the prime minister fully understood the implications of his decisions. The arrival of Green in his influential position caused Diefenbaker to harden his attitude against nuclear weapons.

Diefenbaker's doubts were heightened by the mail his office was receiving from disarmament advocates belonging to groups such as the Voice of Women, who were proud that Canada had been the only country capable of arming itself with nuclear weapons that had chosen not to do so. The influence of the disarmament movement was enlarged by growing concern about the environmental effects of nuclear tests in the atmosphere and the worsening international situation that followed the Soviet Union's shooting down of the American U-2 spy plane piloted by Francis Gary Powers. After Kennedy took office, Soviet Premier Nikita Khrushchev also tested Western resolve in Berlin in the crisis that climaxed with the building of the Berlin Wall. In the face of the competing calls for and against taking nuclear weapons, Diefenbaker chose to delay.

The two meetings in 1961 underlined the personal estrangement between Diefenbaker and Kennedy, and so did Diefenbaker's resistance to nuclear weapons, which complicated negotiations over Canada's acquisition of the F-101 Voodoos. The two sides also differed over American pressure to get Canada to join the Organization of American States, Canada's active trading relationship with communist China and Cuba, and American support of the British move to join the European Common Market, which Canada opposed because it would undermine the Commonwealth trading relationship with Britain.

Although Diefenbaker didn't know it, the question of nuclear weapons for the Bomarcs was about to become much more serious, and he would no longer be able to delay the tough decisions on nuclear arms.

~◦)C◦~

CHAPTER 36

The Bomarc Crisis

JOHN DIEFENBAKER CALLED a federal election for June 18, 1962, and he had hoped to gain support by highlighting his growing differences with the U.S. government. But the election coincided with a financial crisis that undermined the value of the Canadian dollar, to Diefenbaker's great embarrassment and political detriment. Diefenbaker, always resentful of President Kennedy's friendship with Liberal leader Mike Pearson, suspected that Kennedy had helped engineer the financial crisis. But Diefenbaker had also frittered away much of the popularity he'd had four years earlier by deferring decisions, including economic decisions that deepened one of the few recessions of the postwar years. The Arrow decision was a rare example of decisiveness by Diefenbaker, but the temporizing over nuclear weapons that followed was more typical. On election night, Diefenbaker's Conservatives lost 92 seats and were reduced to minority status with 116 seats to 100 for the Liberals, 30 for Social Credit and 19 for Tommy Douglas' NDP.

Although the Arrow cancellation was not an issue discussed in the election, it no doubt cost the Conservatives votes and played a role in their losing a number of Toronto-area ridings, including Peel, where the Avro Canada plant was located. Regardless of the motives of voters, the election left Diefenbaker and his Conservatives in a vulnerable position, forced to deal with other parties to stay in office.

That fall, Kennedy and Khrushchev became embroiled in the most dangerous confrontation of the Cold War, the Cuban Missile Crisis. The crisis unfolded over the final two weeks of October and mounted as Kennedy set up a naval blockade against Soviet ships heading to Cuba. The crisis ended when Khrushchev agreed to stop shipping nuclear-armed missiles to Fidel Castro's Cuba and remove those already there, in exchange for American promises to remove some American missiles located near the Soviet Union and to refrain from invading Cuba.

During the crisis, Kennedy asked Canada for diplomatic support in the United Nations and other forums, and for military co-operation as he put his armed forces on a footing for nuclear war, but Diefenbaker resisted the president's requests. Defence Minister Harkness allowed the Canadian military to covertly raise its alert status while Diefenbaker delayed making a formal decision. While Diefenbaker offered support for the president, it was often qualified, reflecting Diefenbaker's dislike for Kennedy and his anger over being consulted about the crisis only at the last moment.

The crisis brought up again the issue of Canada's preparedness for such a military emergency and Diefenbaker's continued prevarication on the issue of arming

Canada's forces with nuclear weapons. By then, the
two RCAF Bomarc bases had been built and the missiles were in place, awaiting warheads. As well, the
RCAF CF-104 Starfighters in Europe were set to be
equipped with nuclear bombs for their assigned role in
NATO, and the CF-101 Voodoos had Genie missiles to
intercept Soviet bombers, but the Genies required
nuclear warheads. Although the navy considered taking nuclear weapons, they never did, but the army had
acquired Honest John rockets that also used nuclear
warheads for deployment in Europe with NATO forces.
In 1962, all these systems were overdue for a decision
authorizing the acquisition of nuclear warheads and for
agreements between Canada and the U.S. dealing with
control of those weapons. But for most Canadians, the
Bomarc missiles symbolized the growing differences
between Diefenbaker and the American government
over nuclear weapons.

Both inside and outside the Conservative Party, the
issue of Diefenbaker's lukewarm support for Kennedy
in the Cuban crisis undermined the prime minister's
leadership. In Washington, the Kennedy administration's patience with Diefenbaker was exhausted. In
the first few weeks of January, the issue of Canada's
attitude to nuclear weapons exploded into a political
crisis. On January 3, an American general retiring
from command of NATO forces in Europe visited
Ottawa and made pointed comments about Canada's
unarmed missiles and aircraft. A few days later, Liberal leader Pearson announced that his party was
reversing its policy and now favoured arming the

Bomarcs and other systems with nuclear weapons. Conservatives boosted their pressure on Diefenbaker to go ahead with arming the Bomarcs as Parliament returned, but the prime minister continued to stall.

After Diefenbaker addressed the House of Commons with a confusing speech on the subject, the U.S. State Department issued a press release stating that a Canadian diplomat called "a frontal attack on the Canadian government for its nuclear policy." Canada recalled its ambassador from Washington, and though Diefenbaker considered calling an election on the issue, he continued to evade taking a clear stand on arming the Bomarcs. The following Sunday, Diefenbaker hosted a Cabinet meeting at his official residence at 24 Sussex Drive in Ottawa that degenerated into shouting and cursing as Harkness and others threatened to quit, and Diefenbaker in his turn mused about resigning. In the end, the Cabinet stayed with the prime minister for the moment, except for Harkness, who resigned. Two days later, on February 5, Diefenbaker's government fell in a non-confidence vote in the House of Commons.

Although Diefenbaker was able to rally most of his party behind him and was able to exhibit his political skills on the hustings in the election campaign that began the next day, it was not enough to save his government. On April 8, Mike Pearson and the Liberals emerged triumphant in the election, though they were denied a majority. The Pearson government quickly reached an agreement with the U.S. on arming the Bomarcs and other weapons, which called for "dual key" operation of the nuclear weapons by American and Canadian officers, since all the nuclear weapons remained the property of the U.S. government despite their use on Canadian-owned missiles or aircraft. The nuclear warheads for the Bomarcs arrived at the end of the year.

One of the harshest critics of Pearson's decision was a Montreal intellectual named Pierre Elliott Trudeau. Two years later, however, Trudeau joined Pearson's Liberals and, in 1968, replaced Pearson as party leader and prime minister. Shortly after taking office, Trudeau ordered a review of Canada's military, which led to a reduction of Canada's military commitments and military spending.

The Bomarcs remained on alert until they were taken out of service in 1972, the same time as the American Bomarcs were retired. By then, the Honest John rockets were retired, and nuclear weapons had been removed from the Canadian Starfighters. The Genies for the Voodoos remained available for use until June 1984, when Canada gave up its only remaining nuclear weapons. The Genies and their warheads left Canada the same week Trudeau stepped down as prime minister. Although Trudeau's antipathy to nuclear weapons contributed to the Canadian government's decision to give them up, changing war doctrines in NATO, including a move away from the Kennedy policy of flexible response, also played a role. Seven years after the last nuclear warheads left Canadian soil, the Cold War ended with the collapse of the Soviet Union.

Many people date the decline of Canada's military to the Trudeau period, but the reductions in Canada's military spending in the Cold War began with Diefenbaker's decisions to wind up the Arrow and replace the aircraft with a cheaper alternative, the Bomarc. Unfortunately, to be effective, the Bomarc required nuclear warheads. Had the Avro Arrow been built and deployed, it would have likely been armed with nuclear-armed missiles, but the nuclear weapons would not have been as essential to the Arrow as they were to the Bomarc.

CHAPTER 37

The Avro Team Moves On

THE 1960S WERE A TIME of rising expectations in Canada and many other parts of the world, and for much of that decade, many of those expectations were met. While the Avro Arrow fell by the wayside, Canadians pursued other dreams such as building Expo '67, the successful World's Fair in Montréal that capped Canada's celebration of its centennial. President Kennedy set an ambitious national goal in 1961 of landing astronauts on the Moon before the decade was over, and the astronauts of Apollo 11 achieved the goal in July 1969. Engineers and aircraft builders in Russia and another team in England and France set out to build supersonic transport aircraft.

Although Canada had left the military aircraft field, it still had an aircraft industry that built smaller transport aircraft and won subcontracting work on larger military projects. Around Canada, engineers were put to work on infrastructure projects such as superhighways, the Montréal Metro and extensions to Toronto's subway system. Skyscrapers rose in Canadian cities, and dams and nuclear power stations were built around the country to power Canada's expanding population and economy.

In the military field, the Soviet Union and the United States built their forces of nuclear weapons based on ICBMs and fleets of submarines carrying missiles with nuclear warheads, as well as the old standby of bombers. Most of these efforts outside of the Communist Bloc involved talent from the disbanded Avro Canada team. Many of the Avro engineers were snapped up by other Canadian aircraft makers such as de Havilland Canada and Canadair, and others joined American aerospace contractors who were building new aircraft, missiles and spacecraft for the U.S. military and government agencies, and for the world's airlines. Some Avro engineers returned home to England. Avro engineers and skilled workers found themselves in work that is too diverse to recount in this book, but the stories of a few Avro engineers help illustrate the level of talent that was lost when the Arrow was cancelled.

Avro's vice-president of engineering, James Floyd, had hoped to save his team when the Arrow was cancelled by lending out their expertise to other aircraft firms or interested agencies until Avro Canada had a new project. One such effort was spearheaded by Jim Chamberlin and Bob Lindley, who contacted NASA, which had been founded four months before the Arrow's cancellation. NASA was established as the successor of NACA, which for 40 years had conducted research advancing aircraft design in America. The Avro engineers had used NACA facilities to test models of the Arrow, and they knew that the new agency had been charged with setting up Project Mercury, which would shoot humans into space.

Chamberlin and Lindley called on NASA officials in Washington to see if the space agency would be interested in a loan of engineers from Avro. After some discussion, the idea of a loan was quashed, but NASA made it known that it was short of engineers and wanted to hire some of the top people from Avro. Lindley and Chamberlin called Avro's engineers to the plant cafeteria and told them about job opportunities with NASA.

Three weeks after the Arrow was cancelled, a plane carrying top NASA officials landed at the Malton airport, and the NASA officials got a look at the five completed Arrows, which had not yet been broken up for scrap. The next day, the NASA team interviewed 100 Avro engineers and offered jobs to 25 of them, including Chamberlin. Lindley didn't apply and opted to remain with Avro until it formally folded. In the months that followed, NASA hired another six Avro engineers, while others, including Lindley, got involved in the U.S. space program when U.S. aerospace firms hired them.

In April 1959, Chamberlin and his 24 Avro colleagues reported to work at NASA's Langley Research Center in Virginia. Langley was home to the Mercury program until a new space centre was set up in Houston, Texas, in 1962. Mercury was such a new program at the time that many of the Avro engineers reported for work the same day as seven recruits who would fly

James A. Chamberlin

the new spacecraft and become famous as America's first astronauts.

Chamberlin, who was born in Kamloops, BC, but was raised in Toronto, was given one of the top jobs in Mercury: head of the engineering division. As such, he was responsible for the office that ensured the Mercury spacecraft's manufacturers built each spacecraft according to NASA's specifications.

On April 12, 1961, the Soviet Union's Yuri Gagarin became the first human to fly in space, and this latest Soviet space "first" inspired President Kennedy to charge NASA with landing astronauts on the Moon in the Apollo program. At the time, Chamberlin was working on making changes to Mercury so that it could fly longer than just a few orbits. Chamberlin decided that Mercury wasn't up to the job and that a whole new spacecraft was needed, so he began designing a new spacecraft that could carry two astronauts. The new spacecraft was named Gemini and would be able to change orbits and allow astronauts to step outside and do space walks in orbit around the Earth. Gemini was also designed to join up with a rocket named Agena that could boost it into higher orbits.

While Chamberlin was designing Gemini, he was also drawn into the arguments raging inside NASA about how to get Apollo to the Moon. Among three competing concepts, the most popular idea was the direct method: put the astronauts in a rocket that would leave the Earth, carry them directly to the lunar surface and then bring them back to Earth. The second idea involved using two rockets to assemble a lunar spacecraft in orbit around the Earth orbit. The assembled vehicle would then head directly to the Moon and bring astronauts home. The third idea, at first the least popular, was called lunar orbit rendezvous. It involved launching a mother ship and small lunar landing craft from Earth into orbit around the Moon. The astronauts would transfer to the landing craft, land on the Moon and then return to the mother ship, which would then bring the astronauts home.

Although the direct method made the most sense at first glance, it had a number of drawbacks: it required a rocket that was much bigger than what would be needed for the other methods, and designing a single spacecraft to do everything would be very difficult, something like designing an amphibious car for a fishing trip. Lunar orbit rendezvous separated the lunar landing tasks from other parts of the flight, such as Earth launch and re-entry, lowered the weight of the spacecraft, and required a smaller booster rocket. Instead of the amphibious car, this concept was like using a car, a boat and a trailer for a fishing trip. But the idea of astronauts having to find and join up with another spacecraft when they were 400,000 kilometres away from home terrified many people in NASA.

An engineer at NASA named John Houbolt was convinced that lunar orbit rendezvous was the best way to go to the Moon, but few people would listen to him. Houbolt's first convert was Jim Chamberlin, and he announced his conversion in a dramatic way. Chamberlin suggested that instead of sending Apollo to the Moon, an improved version of his Gemini spacecraft could be launched on a Saturn rocket along with a "bug" that could carry a single astronaut to the lunar surface. Although his boss, Robert Gilruth, ordered Chamberlin to halt his work on Gemini lunar flights, he admitted that Chamberlin had made a convincing argument for lunar orbit rendezvous.

Soon Gilruth and others joined the ranks of NASA engineers in favour of lunar orbit rendezvous. In July 1962, NASA announced that it would use that method to get Apollo to the Moon and back. It set to work building a mother ship—the command and service module—to carry three astronauts to lunar orbit and back to Earth, and a smaller craft—the lunar module—that would carry two of them to the surface of the Moon and back to lunar orbit. Jim Chamberlin had played a key role in one of the most important, and most expensive, decisions in NASA's history.

Chamberlin was named manager for the Gemini program, but Gemini soon came up against a set of technical and budgetary challenges, many of them caused by arbitrary cutbacks to Gemini's budget. The Gemini design marked a number of advances from Mercury and would allow astronauts to do many things in Earth orbit that were impossible with Mercury. Chamberlin stepped down as Gemini manager in 1963, but the Gemini spacecraft he designed saw American astronauts seize the lead in the 1960s space race, with space walks, long duration flights and the first rendezvous and docking in space. A total of 10 Gemini flights in 1965 and 1966 proved techniques and prepared astronauts and flight controllers for the challenges of Apollo. When Gemini ended, Chamberlin received a medal from NASA for his contributions to its successes.

After Gemini, Chamberlin worked as a trouble-shooter in the Apollo program, helping NASA management deal with problems affecting the Apollo lunar module, Saturn booster rocket, and even the space suits used in the first lunar landing. Chamberlin went on to make contributions to the shuttle program, and he received more recognition from NASA for his work in these programs.

Of the 31 former Avro engineers hired by NASA in 1959 and 1960, the majority came from the UK and only a dozen were Canadian. Prominent British members of the group included John Hodge, who became one of the first flight directors for NASA alongside legendary figures such as Chris Kraft and Gene Kranz; Rod Rose, who played a key role in drawing up flight plans for the Apollo missions, and Peter Armitage, who worked on recovery systems for Mercury, Gemini and Apollo. Dennis Fielder, George Harris and Tecwyn Roberts worked with Hodge and Canadians Fred Matthews and Eugene Duret on setting up NASA's flight control rooms and worldwide tracking network for Mercury, Gemini and Apollo. The British members of what many people called the "NASA Canadians" even formed a NASA cricket team that played a handful of games in the early 1960s.

The Canadians who worked in Apollo included Bryan Erb, a Calgarian who played a key role in designing Apollo's heat shield; Leonard Packham, a Saskatchewan-born engineer who helped design Apollo's communications systems; computer experts Stanley Cohn and Stanley Galezowski; structures expert Robert Vale; and heating expert George Watts. Richard Carley went from his groundbreaking design work on the Arrow's partially automatic fly-by-wire control system to building control systems for Gemini, Apollo and the shuttle. Bruce Aikenhead helped train the Mercury astronauts and worked on NASA's tracking network. Later, Aikenhead returned to Canada and worked on a number of pioneering Canadian space efforts, including early satellites, the Canadarm for the space shuttle and Canada's astronaut program. After retiring from NASA in the 1980s, Erb joined the Canadian Space Agency and helped develop Canada's contribution to the International Space Station, the Mobile Servicing System.

Owen Maynard, a native of Sarnia, Ontario, was one of the first people employed in the Apollo program, and there he worked on the early design of the Apollo command and service modules. Working with Chamberlin, Maynard helped sell the concept of lunar orbit rendezvous around NASA and was the first person in the space agency to work on the design of the lunar module. In 1964, he became chief of systems engineering in the Apollo program office, where he was in charge of the integration of Apollo systems. As chief of mission operations in 1966 and 1967 before returning to systems engineering, Maynard was one of the key managers in the Apollo program. Maynard left NASA in 1970 after the first two Moon landings and pursued work in the private sector before he returned to Canada upon his retirement.

Just as Maynard was leaving NASA, Bob Lindley joined the agency after a decade of working for McDonnell Aircraft in aircraft programs and with his friend Chamberlin in Gemini, where McDonnell was prime contractor. At NASA, Lindley helped bring the shuttle program to fruition and later helped establish Spacelab, Europe's contribution to the shuttle program.

The Avro engineers made a big contribution to the success of NASA's early human space programs, and Robert Gilruth later described the Avro engineers as a "godsend" for NASA. They certainly played a key role in helping NASA land Apollo astronauts on the Moon on six flights from 1969 to 1972.

Avro engineers also made their presence felt elsewhere. Not long after the Arrow program ended, the Hawker Siddeley group in England summoned James Floyd to work on its proposals for a supersonic transport aircraft (SST). Floyd had already been working on SST concepts for Avro Canada, and when he returned to England, he joined Hawker Siddeley's Advanced Projects Group, bringing with him Avro Canada engineers Pat Mackenzie, Colin Marshall, Ken Cooke, Joe Farbridge, John Morris and John McCulloch. Before the end of 1959, Floyd's group had completed a preliminary design for an advanced SST, but British authorities chose a competing bid from the British Aircraft Corporation. Later, the British and French governments agreed to work jointly on an SST that became known as the Concorde, and British Aircraft worked with Sud Aviation in France to design and build the aircraft, which first flew in 1969.

Floyd formed his own consulting firm in 1962, and he served as a consultant to the British government on Concorde. Although a Soviet SST flew shortly before the Concorde, the British-French aircraft was the only commercially successful SST, flying passengers from 1976 until its retirement in 2003. Floyd returned to Canada in 1980, and he has won many honours for his pioneering work in aviation.

As for the pilots who flew the Arrow, three moved on to test-pilot jobs in the United States, Spud Potocki worked for North American Aviation and Peter Cope test flew airliners for Boeing.

The lone RCAF pilot who flew the Arrow, Jack Woodman, was put to work evaluating new aircraft for the RCAF. When the government chose the F-104 Starfighter for the RCAF in Europe, Woodman was assigned to work at the Lockheed plant in Palmdale, California, to prepare for the production of CF-104s. The American firm offered Woodman a job, and he retired from his Squadron Leader position in the RCAF in 1962 and joined Lockheed.

Before Canada got its first astronauts in 1983, Woodman was probably the closest thing Canada had to an astronaut. While in the RCAF, according to the Canadian Aviation Hall of Fame, "Woodman was at the top of an unofficial list of three or four RCAF pilots who were possible candidates for the U.S. space program as astronauts." Such a chance never came, but at Lockheed, Woodman became project pilot on the NF-104A Aerospace Trainer, a modified Starfighter designed to fly to the edge of space. On one flight, Woodman took the aircraft more than 36 kilometres high, an unofficial altitude record for the time. The same aircraft was flown by famed U.S. test pilot Chuck Yeager in a flight that nearly cost him his life, and the incident was immortalized in a sequence in the 1983 movie *The Right Stuff.* During his two decades with Lockheed, Woodman flew many other aircraft, especially the L1011 airliner.

Jan Zurakowski could have found work in the United States, too, but he had already retired from active test flying when the Arrow was cancelled, and he decided to leave aviation altogether. Zurakowski established a summer resort, Kartuzy Lodge, near Barry's Bay, Ontario. He spent the rest of his life running the lodge, occasionally attending reunions of the Avro team or accepting honours for his work as a test pilot. Probably the honour that was most meaningful was being named, in 2000, an Honorary Fellow of the Society of Experimental Test Pilots, alongside such flying legends as Charles Lindbergh, Jimmy Doolittle, Igor Sikorski and Sir Frank Whittle.

~୭C~

CHAPTER 38

The Arrow's Afterlife

EXCEPT FOR THE ODD magazine and newspaper article or radio discussion, most Canadians heard little about the Avro Arrow in the 1960s. Although the decade gave Canadians new dreams to pursue, the expectations raised in that tumultuous time grew to the point where they became impossible to meet. And though Canada escaped much of the 1960s tumult that had struck the United States and Europe, many people began to question governments and large institutions in ways that had not been done before. The American Civil Rights Movement opposed the institutionalized racism found in many parts of the U.S., and the Anti-war Movement stood against the war in Vietnam. Other movements questioned the roles of universities, governments and technology, advocated for the rights of women and minority groups, and spoke out against degradation of the environment.

These movements spawned a counterculture that questioned modern society's reliance on technology, especially technology linked to nuclear war and other military purposes. This criticism of technology ultimately shot down the technological aspirations that followed in the path of the Arrow. It helped bring the Apollo Moon program to an early end and dashed NASA's dreams of sending humans to Mars in the 20th century. As well, questions about sonic booms and other environmental impacts of supersonic transports caused the U.S. Senate to end funding for an American SST and limit the use of the Concorde SST. Criticism of military priorities led to reductions in military budgets in Canada and, to a lesser extent, in the U.S.

Although the 1960s movements originated in the United States, many Canadians were inspired by their messages. Some Canadians became strong nationalists, but the 1960s had their strongest effects in Québec, where the so-called Quiet Revolution saw Québeckers turn away from the Catholic Church and toward the welfare state. Many Québeckers also become separatists and created a movement that remained strong into the 21st century.

The 1970s brought an end to the long postwar boom that Canadians and Americans had enjoyed, dashing many dreams. And as the Baby Boom generation born in the postwar era came of age, its large numbers made the ambitions of many of its members impossible to fulfill.

As Canada's economy sputtered in the 1970s amid growing concerns about foreign takeovers of Canadian firms and resources, many Canadians began to ask where the hopes of the postwar period had foundered. Some people recalled how Canada had become an industrial powerhouse during World War II, and how the promise of that time had faded as the Canadian economy persisted in its dependence on extraction of resources such as timber, minerals and gas and oil. Although the auto industry provided many jobs in Ontario and Québec, Canadians seemed to be missing out on manufacturing and high-tech jobs that could be found in parts of the U.S., Europe and Japan.

As concerned Canadians questioned where their economy had gone wrong, some began to look at the fate of the Avro Arrow. In 1978, the first of a number of books decrying the fate of the Arrow began to appear, with Murray Peden's *Fall of an Arrow*, which denounced Diefenbaker's cancellation of the Arrow program and called the destruction of the five completed aircraft an "appalling act of vandalism." The following year, E. Kay Shaw's *There Never Was an Arrow*, critiqued Diefenbaker's actions from a Canadian nationalist perspective. Shaw was an engineering technologist who was one of the few women to hold such a position at Avro Canada. The same year, James Dow wrote *The Arrow*, which remains one of the best accounts of the program, and the Canadian Broadcasting Corporation produced an hour-long program called *There Never Was an Arrow*. The show, which was not broadcast until after the 1980 federal election, resurrected many of the controversies that surrounded the Arrow. Also in 1980, four people who were involved in the Arrow program, and who called themselves the Arrowheads, put out a colourful book, *Avro Arrow: The Story of the Avro Arrow from its Evolution to its Extinction*, which contained photos, diagrams and charts, along with many recollections of the CF-105. The book became a Canadian publishing phenomenon and remains in print today.

These works rekindled the national discussion about the Arrow and raised the profile of what some critics have called a "cult" around the Arrow. This discussion also brought out critics, notably Desmond Morton, the distinguished Canadian historian, who wrote in a 1986 *Toronto Star* article on the anniversary of Black Friday that the Arrow was a "fatally flawed weapon on a par with those earlier monuments to our military-industrial blundering, the Ross rifle or the MacAdam shovel [both controversially produced in World War I]."

When Greig Stewart completed his popular work on the Arrow, *Shutting Down the National Dream*, in 1989, historian Michael Bliss launched an unrelenting attack on Avro in the *Report on Business Magazine*: "It's time to bury the tarnished, unhistorical, untrue myth of the Avro men and their flying machines. Diefenbaker's pricking of Avro's fantasies was one of his government's most responsible acts."

Stewart's book was followed in 1992 by Palmiro Campagna's *Storms of Controversy: The Secret Avro Arrow Files Revealed*, which contained new information about the Arrow program and strongly defended it against its critics. Campagna wrote that he believed the country as a whole was affected psychologically by the Arrow cancellation.

The Arrow began appearing in novels, and in 1990, playwright Clinton Bomphray put on a production of his play, *The Legend of the Avro Arrow*, at the National Arts Centre in Ottawa.

"In a country that is still too young to have birthed many legends, it's one of the first ones, I think, that's springing to life," Bomphray told CBC-TV reporter Susan Harada, comparing the Arrow to the mythical sword of Excalibur. "The idea occurred to us that there was comparison with the King Arthur legend, where Arthur wrested Excalibur the sword from the rock, the land of Great Britain, in order to unite the people and defend it from invaders. Similarly, the Arrow was wrested from the rock of Canada by the Canadian people and held aloft to defend us from invaders, and unite us as a people. And in that legend, eventually Excalibur was thrown into the lake at the end of the story. And so we threw the Arrow into our figurative lake, the junkyard in Hamilton."

Bomphray said he was trying to compare the Arrow to other Canadian national symbols such as the Mounted Police, Canada's grain elevators and the *Bluenose*. The Arrow, he said, opened to Canada the possibility for an independent military, an independent foreign policy and an independent manufacturing policy.

A critic of the play, Carleton University Classics professor A. Trevor Hodge, noted in an interview that the play appeared at an emotional time for Canadian nationalism, shortly after the Conservative government of Brian Mulroney brought in Free Trade with the United States and attempted to deal with Québec's aspirations with the equally controversial and ultimately unsuccessful Meech Lake Accord.

In the late 1970s, the Arrow had taken to the air again, this time at the heart of a new national myth. As the 1990s continued, the myth of the Arrow reached new heights.

CHAPTER 39

The Miniseries and the Models

IN THE FIRST DAYS OF January 1997, Canadians could have beeen forgiven for thinking they had stepped into a 40-year time warp featuring the Avro Arrow. The Arrow appeared in newspapers and on the cover of *Maclean's* magazine and TV program guides. Experts argued the merits of the Arrow on television and radio and in editorial pages. The aircraft's step back into the limelight was the result of a miniseries called *The Arrow* that appeared over two nights on CBC-TV. The miniseries featured Dan Aykroyd, a Canadian comedian who had found fame in Hollywood, and who agreed to return to television and his home country to play former Avro Canada President Crawford Gordon in a retelling of the Arrow story. CBC spent more than $7 million on the miniseries, and it has since been replayed many times on television and is available on videocassette and DVD.

At a preview screening, James Floyd, who headed up the technical work on the Arrow, and former Avro test pilot Jan Zurakowski, said they were relieved that the miniseries was labelled "dramatic fiction" because it departed from the true story in many respects. For example, Jack Woodman's role in testing the Arrow is exaggerated at the expense of Zurakowski and Spud Potocki. Although Floyd is accounted for in the miniseries, Jim Chamberlin is depicted as the main designer who comes up with important firsts for the Arrow. Not only was Chamberlin's importance in Avro exaggerated, his character was changed for dramatic effect. Also, a systems expert, Kate O'Hara, was an invented character. "The show got the technicalities wrong quite a bit," Zurakowski commented.

Although Aykroyd was praised for his depiction of Gordon, and television host Elwy Yost, who worked for Avro in the personnel department before going into broadcasting, pronounced the show "splendid," others criticized the miniseries for its anti-American tone and for depicting Diefenbaker as the villain of the story. The miniseries ends with the greatest of Arrow legends, that one of the Arrows took to the skies after Black Friday and escaped the wrecker's saws.

Perhaps the most interesting story to come out of the miniseries concerns the other star of the piece, a full-scale replica of the Arrow that was used to re-create the rollout ceremony at Malton on the day *Sputnik* was launched. The rollout was re-enacted at a Winnipeg air museum in the summer of 1996. The replica Arrow had not been expressly built for the miniseries but was the labour of love of a sales estimator from Wetaskiwin, Alberta.

The replica's creator was a man named Allan Jackson, who in the 1950s followed the Arrow story and hoped to work building such planes when he completed his education. The Arrow was cancelled while Jackson attended the Southern Alberta Institute of Technology in Calgary, and his career went in other directions. In the 1980s, he purchased a book about the Arrow, and in 1990, he began to build on a full-scale replica. Jackson, who worked for a steel fabrication firm, started with the plane's cockpit, which he built from wood and fibreglass. Next, he went on to build the rest of the fuselage. By early 1996, he was working on the wings, and he had completed roughly seven-tenths of the replica when the producers of the miniseries contacted him. They hired a crew to complete the work, and Jackson looked on with pride as his replica played its starring role in the recreation of the rollout at Malton.

Then history repeated itself. The replica was used in a scene depicting the destruction of the Arrows, and this scene involved too much realism for Jackson's liking. "I didn't expect them to destroy my components," he told Gerry Bellett of the *Vancouver Sun*. "They used cutting torches to cut steel spars into three pieces. I couldn't believe the damage they'd done." Jackson spent eight months repairing the damage, and his Arrow model was fixed in time to star in the 1997 Abbotsford Air Show in BC's Fraser Valley. Tens of thousands of aircraft fans who had seen the miniseries earlier that year crowded around the replica.

The Arrow mock-up was returned to Wetaskiwin, a city just south of Edmonton that is home to the Reynolds Alberta Museum, which contains a large collection of cars, trucks, farm equipment and aircraft. Next

Arrow replica at the 1997 Abbotsford Air Show

~∞✕∞~

to the museum is the permanent home of the Canadian Aviation Hall of Fame, where many of the individuals who helped create and fly the Avro Arrow and other historic Canadian aircraft are enshrined. The replica was stored outside for a time and sustained some damage, but today it is fully restored and is displayed in a large warehouse with other historic aircraft.

The same year the model appeared in Abbotsford, a group of aviation enthusiasts in Toronto opened the Toronto Aviation Museum in a hangar that once was part of the de Havilland Canada plant, in an area of the Toronto suburb of Downsview that is being converted into a park. The following year, some of the people who volunteered at the museum, including some who had formerly worked at Avro, decided to build a full-sized replica of their own. For eight years, a dedicated team of volunteers at the museum, with help from local aviation firms who supplied components, services and materials, designed and assembled a full-scale reproduction of the third Arrow, which was unveiled in a weekend of celebrations in October 2006—49 years after the original Arrow had been rolled out.

Avro Arrow enthusiasts have a major presence on the Internet, with a number of websites dedicated to preserving the memory of the Arrow, the Jetliner and the Avrocar. The Aerospace Heritage Foundation of Canada is an organization created to preserve mementos of Canadian aviation, particularly the Arrow. Another group of Arrow enthusiasts has been searching the bottom of Lake Ontario for scale models of the Arrow that were launched atop rockets to test the aircraft's flying characteristics, and in 2004, it enlisted the Canadian Navy to help with its as-yet unsuccessful search. Another group spearheaded by Peter Zuuring hoped to create a full-scale flying replica of the Arrow to celebrate the centennial of flight in Canada in 2009. Zuuring created two interesting books and other publications, and carried out research that turned up a number of previously unknown documents, and even an Iroquois engine in England. But his plans for a flying replica appear to have fallen short.

Arrow relics are popular attractions in aircraft museums around Canada, and the nose sections of Arrow 6 and the Jetliner are popular draws at the Canadian Aviation Museum at Rockcliffe near Ottawa.

Caps, T-shirts, prints, models, videos and other souvenirs of the Arrow always sell well at these museums.

Fifty years after the Arrow first appeared on a tarmac, the aircraft remains a vivid memory for many Canadians, many of whom still ask, "Who killed the Arrow?" and "Why did they do it?"

PART 2:

Who Killed The Arrow?

CHAPTER 40

The United States

MANY ELEMENTS WENT INTO the demise of the Avro Arrow, including mounting costs, the changing military threat to Canada and the U.S. in the late 1950s, the political situation in Canada, and the prospect of selling the Arrow and making it less expensive to produce. Many people brush by these difficult and complex matters, and simply ask, what did the United States have to do with the end of the Arrow? Did the American government push the Canadian government to cancel the Arrow? By refusing to buy the Arrow, did the U.S. doom the aircraft?

The relationship between the U.S. and Canadian militaries is complex, and these complexities must be considered in the case of the Avro Arrow. The Arrow was of more than a casual interest to the U.S. military because, had it been brought into service, it would have formed an integral part of the nation's defence against Soviet bombers. Had the Soviet Union chosen to dispatch bombers to strike the U.S., nearly all of them would have had to pass over or near Canadian airspace. Although a few of these bombers might have been directed against targets in Canada, most of their targets would have been inside the United States.

As part of its defensive efforts, the U.S. government signed agreements with Canada to set up radars including the Pinetree Line, the Mid-Canada Line and the DEW Line. The U.S. also had radars operating in Alaska, Greenland and Europe. Because of Canada's position between the two Cold War adversaries, the U.S. sought to negotiate an agreement with Canada that provided for integrated command of air forces through NORAD to protect both countries against Soviet attack. Although the Conservatives signed the NORAD agreement shortly after they took office in 1957, the Liberals were also prepared to sign the agreement, and the NORAD agreement has been renewed several times and remains in force 50 years after it came into effect, long outliving the Cold War that inspired its creation. During the life of NORAD, the interdependence between the two militaries was demonstrated on more than one occasion. For example, the Canadian military quietly raised its alert status, over the objections of the prime minister, in the Cuban Missile Crisis of 1962, and nearly 40 years later, the Canadian deputy commander happened to be in charge of NORAD's combat operations when terrorists attacked the U.S. on September 11, 2001.

The Arrow would have been an asset to the United States' defence as well as Canada's. Indeed, the USAF and American agencies such as NACA provided the RCAF and Avro Canada with information about aerodynamics and access to wind tunnel facilities at NACA facilities at Langley Aeronautical Laboratory in Virginia and the Lewis Flight Propulsion Laboratory in Cleveland, Ohio.

As part of the Arrow trials, Avro acquired U.S. Nike rockets and launched them to test the aerodynamic characteristics of the Arrow models, and some of these launches took place from U.S. launch sites.

The USAF gave a B-47 to the RCAF to test the Iroquois engine and trained the Avro test pilots who flew it. Avro test pilots such as Jan Zurakowski also gained experience flying delta-winged aircraft courtesy of the USAF. And on top of everything else, the U.S. government gave its Canadian allies access to technology built by American aerospace firms in the form of weapons fire-control systems and Falcon missiles, amongst other things, that were being installed on the Arrow. The Arrow would have been useless as a weapons system without the help of U.S. contractors.

If the U.S. government had wanted to block the Arrow, it most likely would not have provided assistance to Avro and the RCAF. But even people who know about this assistance have suggested that the U.S. tried to halt the Arrow.

In *Storms of Controversy*, Palmiro Campagna floated the idea that late in 1958, some Americans came to feel threatened by the CF-105, which could potentially shoot down the U-2 reconnaissance aircraft—America's primary source of information on the strength of the Soviet military. The U-2's work in Soviet airspace ended in 1960 when the Soviet Air Force shot one down a few months before the first

U.S. reconnaissance satellite program, which was known as CORONA, had its first successful flight. With the Arrow cancelled, the U.S., and particularly the Central Intelligence Agency (CIA), in the words of Campagna, "would be able to breathe a sigh of relief, and Canada would *never again* be involved in the high altitude interceptor game...Having been so closely involved [in the Arrow] and having been told the project's vulnerabilities, the United States would have known that the simple refusal to purchase the aircraft, combined with the insistence to set up the Bomarcs, would be enough to kill [the Arrow]. In this way, the Bomarcs would be installed, the Arrow terminated, the manufacturing data (already in American hands) already destroyed, the U-2 program protected, and the Canadians even willing to throw in their brilliant engineers and technicians for the avaricious prospect of obtaining lucrative deals in the United States. The Americans had everything to gain, and did."

Although Americans and Canadians have their differences, Canada's small population and economic power relative to America's might dictates friendship. "The Americans are our best friends, whether we like it or not," as Canadian politician Robert Thompson once put it. Although the two countries can and do differ in international organizations and have trade disputes that sometimes cause angry words and provocative actions, a military breach between the two is almost unthinkable.

The matter of trade brings the Arrow into a matter of running contention between the U.S. and Canada.

Simply put, Canada offered to sell the Arrow to the U.S., and the U.S. refused on a number of occasions. Had the U.S. or another country bought the Arrow, more aircraft could have been produced and the cost to Canadian taxpayers would have been reduced, giving Ottawa a reason to press on with the Arrow instead of cancelling it.

There are a number of reasons the U.S. didn't buy the Arrow. For one, they, as a rule, don't buy large aircraft such as the Arrow from foreign countries. In two cases, the U.S. opted for foreign aircraft to fill a unique niche, and in both cases the aircraft were built in the United States under licence. The first was the English Electric Canberra, which filled a need for an all-weather jet bomber early in the 1950s, and the USAF used Canberras built in the U.S. by Martin. The other case was the Harrier Jump Jet, the one-of-a-kind VTOL aircraft that was produced in Britain by Hawker Aircraft and its successors and was later made in the U.S. by McDonnell Douglas.

Although the U.S. military bought some aircraft such as the de Havilland Canada Caribou to fill specialized needs, large aircraft procurements have always involved American firms. One reason for this will be familiar to anyone who observes trade disputes between the U.S. and Canada: the United States Congress. Members of Congress are not often compelled to look at the national interest because executive and legislative functions are separated in the American system, but they require local support to get elected. This makes members of Congress tenacious advocates for their home states and districts in matters such as government procurement and, as Canadians know only too well, matters such as lumber and wood production. Many powerful members of Congress, such as former Speaker Newt Gingrich and former House Minority Leader Dick Gephardt, to name just two, had major aerospace plants in their districts and worked hard to keep them in production. Often programs are continued to keep plants and jobs coming, even when the product is no longer needed or is of questionable effectiveness. No votes were to be had from buying aircraft from Canada.

Another reason why American military aircraft procurement is kept at home is the American system of subsidizing its civil aircraft programs through military work. European countries and, in recent years Canada, have provided direct subsidies to support civilian aircraft manufacturers. The U.S. does not provide direct subsidies but instead indirectly subsidizes civilian aircraft projects through military contracts. Boeing aircraft developed many of the technologies it needed for its jet transports while building the B-47, and its first jet airliner, the 707, was also first built for the USAF as a tanker aircraft, the KC-135. With congressional patronage and the role of military contracts in the health of America's aircraft industry, the incentives to build aircraft in the U.S. are strong.

There are other reasons the U.S. did not buy the Arrow. They had developed similar aircraft of their own, and in the late 1950s, the USAF was developing the North American F-108 Rapier, a delta-winged aircraft that would have had a larger combat radius than the Arrow. But it was cancelled a few months after the Arrow was cancelled—because emphasis was shifting to ICBMs and away from bombers. For similar reasons, Britain and other countries were cancelling their own jet interceptor programs, which made the Arrow even more difficult to sell.

Another factor working against the Arrow—as writers such as Dow and others have pointed out—is that the aircraft was designed for Canadian needs, which limited its attraction to foreign buyers. The very logic that led the RCAF to ask Avro to build a special aircraft for its use limited its value on the foreign arms market.

The widely publicized attempts by Defence Minister George Pearkes to sell the Arrow may have been just another effort to foreshadow and justify the cancellation of the program because, for the reasons outlined above, a positive reply was most unlikely.

And then there's the question of timing. James Floyd has argued that the Arrow could only have been sold to other nations once it had been fully developed. "No foreign aircraft has been bought by any country before the country offering it has equipped its own forces with it and proved its effectiveness in squadron use," Floyd wrote.

Another element that fuels controversy about the United States' attitude towards the Arrow concerns their response to the Canadian sales pitches for the plane—the offer of Bomarc missiles and aircraft such as the F-101 Voodoo at fire-sale prices. Critics of the Arrow cancellation suggest that these offers undermined the Arrow and eased the way for its cancellation. Evidence strongly supports this idea, but motives for the American's actions remain open for debate. Fred Smye's trip to Washington late in 1958 to save the Arrow, which he said produced an American offer to help pay for the aircraft, raises the question of whether Washington simply wanted to make sure Canada had interceptors to deploy against Soviet bombers, regardless of where the planes came from.

But controversy continues to surround the Bomarc missiles' role in the Arrow's demise, given that not long after Canada cancelled the Arrow, the USAF began to distance itself from the Bomarc and even suggested that it be cancelled. The Bomarc program continued, and the missile was deployed in the U.S. as well as Canada, but in reduced numbers. Problems with the Bomarc may have been one of the reasons that Canada opted to take the F-101 Voodoo when the U.S. government offered it. As Diefenbaker ruefully put it in his memoirs: "Our decision to introduce the Bomarc did not work out well. To begin with, the Bomarc was very soon proven to be virtually obsolete, even before it was set up." Despite the questions surrounding the Bomarc, the USAF did put the missile into service for more than a decade, even as it cancelled other programs such as the F-108.

Finally, the demise of the Arrow and subsequent developments in Canadian arms procurement bring into question the Defence Production Sharing Agreements between Canada and the United States. These agreements began in World War II and have since been broadened by both Liberal and Conservative governments. The 1959 agreement that followed the Arrow's cancellation deepened the relationship and had the effect of formalizing Canada's role as a builder of components for American defence contractors. Never again would a Canadian firm build a major military system like the Arrow or the CF-100 as prime contractor. Boosters of the agreement state that it gave Canadian contractors greater access to American military work, somewhat in the same manner as the Auto Pact between the two nations, signed in 1965, formalized arrangements in that industry, opening the door for Canadian firms to make more money than they would have servicing only the Canadian market. But as with every trade agreement signed between the two countries, including the 1988 Free Trade Agreement and its successor, the North American Free Trade Agreement, many Canadians ask, with reason, whether the U.S. used its economic strength to bully Canada into a bad deal.

Many Canadians view the Arrow as Canada's last chance, as playwright Clinton Bomphray did, for military and foreign policies independent of the United States. In truth, those options had been foreclosed long before the Arrow was cancelled. The Arrow itself would never have gone as far as it did without U.S. collaboration. Built with the assistance of American contractors and researchers, and containing systems built in the U.S., the Arrow was a symbol of interdependence of the Canadian and American militaries in the Cold War world.

CHAPTER 41

There Never Was an Arrow

How much was the Arrow at fault for its own demise? To supporters of the Arrow, this most provocative question, must be addressed. Critics such as Desmond Morton and Michael Bliss have raised the issue of flaws they believed were built into the aircraft. Morton, for example, charged in his 1986 *Toronto Star* article that lowering missiles out of the weapons bay just before firing would cause the Arrow to "self-destruct." Morton's claim was strongly contested by the Avro engineers, and no other critic has ever raised that point, so that makes it questionable at best.

Engineers associated with the National Research Council's high-speed aerodynamics laboratory have also criticized the Arrow. Avro engineers got into a dispute with NRC engineers over the Arrow's aerodynamics qualities. This disagreement has gained something of a legendary status among the Avro engineers, and Bryan Erb's account of the story appeared earlier in this book. The dispute was brought to American aerodynamicists at NACA and was settled in favour of the Avro design. Although engineers from the NRC have criticized the Arrow's military role, cost and economics, they refrain from criticizing it for serious technical failings.

The flight testing done on the Arrow in 1958 and 1959 had not encountered major problems with the aircraft. But there were problems with the Arrow's landing gear and with handling. The Arrow's fly-by-wire system required a great deal more work, and the aircraft's problems with sideslip made it a challenge to fly. This meant that the Arrow was far from the point where RCAF pilots without extensive flight test experience could fly it. The Arrow had not yet been flown with the Iroquois engine, which itself still required a year of development before it could be produced on a large scale. On the day it was terminated, the Arrow had a total of 70 hours in the air, and it would have needed at least 1000 hours before it could be put into service.

The timing of the Arrow's termination lies behind a great deal of the bad feeling around the decision. To those unfamiliar with the aircraft business, the Arrow's 11 months of flight testing suggested that the aircraft was almost ready to be put into production and into service. In fact, the flight testing was still in its early stages, and on the day the Arrow was cancelled, the aircraft was still nearly three years away from entering flight service.

Another critic of the Arrow, Trevor Hodge, wrote: "The Arrow was a warplane, a military weapon. What would have happened if the Arrow had in fact succeeded and been sold around the world as planned?

[I]t would have been in good time to figure in the Vietnam War. Vietnamese villages napalmed by Canadian Arrows? Is that something we would want to boast about?"

Hodge was wrong about Vietnam, because the Arrow was not the type of aircraft that would have been useful to the U.S. or Vietnamese militaries in that war. But he did raise a point that is often forgotten by people who have been struck by the Arrow's sleek lines: the Arrow was a weapons system built to intercept and shoot down Soviet bombers. This meant that the Arrow would have been fitted with weapons such as Hawk air-to-air missiles, or the Genie air-to-air missile, which was used by RCAF CF-101 Voodoo interceptors. The weapons fire-control system that had caused so much trouble hadn't yet been installed in the Arrow and could not be fully tested until the Arrow flew with its weapons pack fitted with missiles. The beginning of this important testing work was still months away when the Arrow met its end.

David Golden, who in 1959 was deputy minister of defence production, told the CBC for its 1980 documentary: "As a fighting instrument of war, which must include an aircraft, an engine and a sophisticated fire-control system, then of course there never was an Arrow." His statement remains one of the most controversial comments about the Arrow, and indeed was used as the title for the documentary. Although blunt, this statement contains a great deal of truth for those who were charged with building

Canada a weapons system that would defend Canada and the U.S. from Soviet bombers.

If it is true that critics such as Morton and Hodge criticized the Arrow to excess, some of the plane's promoters have strayed even farther from the truth in praising it. The ideas that exaggerate the Arrow's capabilities got their most public airing in the mini-series *The Arrow*, in which Jim Chamberlin is depicted personally inventing many of the ideas that advanced jet technology in the 1950s, such as the area rule, when in fact those advanced concepts were invented elsewhere and used on other aircraft that came before the Arrow. At Avro, he worked under other talented people such as Robert Lindley and James Floyd. Chamberlin's greatest contributions to engineering came after he left Avro and went to NASA. The mini-series also suggested that the Arrow was the most advanced aircraft of its day, another exaggeration. The Arrow was certainly state of the art, and its fly-by-wire control system broke new ground, but there were other aircraft produced at the time that were comparable or even better.

Canadian aviation author Larry Milberry wrote that the U.S. funded more ambitious interceptor projects in the 1950s, including the Republic XF-91 Thunderceptor, the XF-103 and the North American F-108, all of which were cancelled. Lockheed worked on the A-12, which was capable of Mach 3.5. Although an interceptor version of this craft never went into production, the aircraft evolved into the legendary SR-71 Blackbird reconnaissance aircraft, which first flew in 1964, could cruise at Mach 3 and served for three decades. Milberry noted that the F-106 Delta Dart could fly at Mach 2.3, and other jets built at roughly the same time as the Arrow could match or exceed its performance, including the French Mirage III and the Soviet MiG-25. Milberry also asserted that the F-101 Voodoo was competitive with the Arrow. According to Julius Lukasiewicz, a former head of NRC's high-speed aerodynamics laboratory, other countries including Argentina and Egypt tried and failed to build their own independent military aviation capabilities in the 1950s. Although Sweden had gained some success in this field, it was becoming increasingly dependent on foreign suppliers to help build military aircraft.

"Particularly in aeronautics, international production and co-production have become the norm," Lukasiewicz wrote in 1986. Events since then have borne out his words: the great aviation firms of Europe, including Dassault, Sud and Hawker Siddeley, merged into national firms such as British Aerospace and then into BAE Systems. French, German and Spanish aerospace firms have merged into one large European conglomerate, the European Aeronautic Defence and Space Company (EADS). EADS and BAE worked together in Airbus, the civilian aircraft builder that is an EADS subsidiary. American aerospace firms have merged into Lockheed Martin, Boeing or Northrop Grumman. Canada's aviation industry has become concentrated in Bombardier, which took over the former operations of

Canadair, de Havilland Canada and the Boeing operations in Canada. Where Avro Canada would have fit into this merged aerospace world had it and the Arrow survived is a matter of pure conjecture.

The Arrow was cancelled at a moment when it had shown that it could fly, and its aesthetic beauty was evident to everyone who saw it. But it was still a long way from proving that it could do the job assigned to it, protecting Canada and the United States from Soviet bombers. And questions remained about how dire the threat posed by bombers actually was as the missile age opened.

CHAPTER 42

The Missile Age

As WAS RECOUNTED EARLIER in this book, the Soviet Union served dramatic notice that the missile age had arrived on the same day that the Avro Arrow was rolled out of its hangar for the first time. By putting the Earth's first artificial satellite, *Sputnik*, into orbit, the Soviets proved beyond a doubt that they had could deliver nuclear bombs anywhere on Earth in just minutes. A year later, the U.S. had successfully tested similar ICBMs, and in the 1960s, missiles became the major means of delivering nuclear warheads, and remained so through the Cold War and beyond.

"Overnight, fears of a 'bomber gap' between a stunned West and the East were replaced with fears of a 'missile gap' as Western intelligence now confirmed that the principal Soviet threat to North America would now come from intercontinental ballistic missiles," historians Russell Isinger and Donald Story wrote. "Accordingly, the strategic rationale behind Western defence began shifting from an emphasis on defence to deterrence."

What this meant is that the whole dynamic of war had changed. Bombers flying between the USSR and Canada or the United States required several hours to reach their targets, and thus they could be defended against by using radars and interceptor aircraft or missiles such as the Bomarc. ICBMs were a whole different matter. They could be launched with the press of a button or the turn of a key, and their nuclear warheads could wreak destruction on targets on the other side of the Earth in a half hour. The deployment of submarine-launched ballistic missiles in the 1960s shortened the time required to deliver nuclear warheads to Cold War adversaries to just a few minutes. On top of everything else, there was no effective defence against ICBMs, and still isn't to this day. (Over the years, the U.S. and Russia have attempted to create systems to defend against ICBMs, most famously in the 1980s with President Ronald Reagan's Strategic Defence Initiative or "Star Wars." Even though the U.S. has a limited missile defence system, which was deployed in 2004, it cannot defend against a large ICBM force such as Russia's.)

Because of ICBMs' speed and the lack of a defence against them, strategic doctrines changed. The focus became deterring the adversary with the promise of a retaliatory strike that would destroy them many times over. Although both the U.S. and the Soviets maintained their bomber fleets, the fact that missiles made possible the completion of an entire nuclear war long before the bombers from one side could reach their targets put the aircraft into a secondary role. For example, the B-52 remained America's major strategic bomber through most of the Cold War, which ended nearly 40 years after the aircraft was built. And markets for interceptors shrank just as the Arrow was first being flown.

At roughly the same time as *Sputnik* was launched, the U-2 spy plane was overflying the Soviet Union and finding that the threat from Soviet bombers such as the M-4 "Bison" and the Tu-95 "Bear" was exaggerated because there were fewer bombers in a state of readiness than had been estimated. Western observers at Soviet air shows had been fooled about the numbers of these bombers when the same set of aircraft flew repeatedly over the reviewing stand. The Soviets had put more resources into ICBMs, and their "first" with *Sputnik* demonstrated their success. Although the Soviet lead in ICBMs in the late 1950s was soon shown to be exaggerated, the Soviets worked hard through the 1960s to match the success Americans were having in the ICBM field at that time.

The result of the ICBM threat was that Canada lived under the American nuclear umbrella, and still does. Although Canada maintained air defences such as the CF-101, the CF-5 and the CF-18, Canada's major contribution to the defence of the West during the Cold War was its air and ground forces in Europe. Because the Arrow was not suited for the strike role designated to Canada's aircraft in Europe, the importance of the Arrow was downgraded, which made it easier for the Diefenbaker government to cancel the plane without affecting Canada's defensive strength.

CHAPTER 43

Budgets and Politics

THE HISTORICAL RECORD shows that Prime Minister John Diefenbaker terminated the CF-105 Avro Arrow on February 20, 1959. But beyond that, the question remains: why did Diefenbaker kill the Arrow? The matter of possible problems with the Arrow, the strategic situation and United States' role in the cancellation have been discussed in the last few pages. But that leaves questions about the politics of the Arrow, its cost and the relationship between Avro Canada and the Canadian government.

First, how responsible was John Diefenbaker for the demise of the Arrow? Many Canadians who believe that the Arrow should have carried on demonize the man who sealed the plane's fate, but the facts suggest that much of this anger is misplaced. The Liberals were preparing to bring the Arrow to a halt had they won the 1957 election instead of the Conservatives, and they did little to hide the fact. As recounted in this book, C.D. Howe was frequently critical of the Arrow, and when Diefenbaker prepared to cancel it, Howe counselled Liberal Leader Mike Pearson not to criticize the decision. Pearson and his colleagues followed Howe's advice, though they did criticize Diefenbaker's handling of the situation. One possibility remains: what if the Liberals had returned as a minority government? Political expediency can sometimes trump other considerations when governments hold minority positions, and the Diefenbaker government's minority status probably kept the Arrow program going 18 months longer than it might otherwise have lasted.

Second, more evidence has emerged in recent years highlighting the role of the Chiefs of Staff, who pushed for cancellation of the Arrow. Although the Chief of Air Staff, Air Marshall Hugh Campbell, did not support the cancellation, he was reluctantly brought into acquiescing to the recommendations of his army and navy colleagues, which went to the Cabinet in August 1958. In the face of those recommendations from Defence Minister Pearkes, soon, he and Diefenbaker were moving toward cancellation. Doubtless a Liberal government would have received a similar recommendation and reacted in a similar way.

Diefenbaker repaid the attacks over the Arrow by overstating the case for cancelling the aircraft. He raised questions of mounting costs and the advent of ICBMs, along with questions about the Arrow's range, questions that the aircraft's defenders always criticized. "Should we go on spending your money as taxpayers to produce the Arrow, which is an attractive aircraft of fine workmanship and design, but which would be out of date when produced?" the prime minister asked a few weeks after cancelling the Arrow.

This claim, the charge that the CF-105 was "potentially useless," inflamed defenders of the aircraft, though it was in reference to the growing ICBM threat rather than the Arrow's rank amongst interceptor aircraft. Diefenbaker's more colourful attacks on the Arrow—"There is no purpose in manufacturing horse collars when horses no long exist"—also poured fuel on the fire.

Despite the lack of evidence tying Diefenbaker to the actual destruction of the Arrows following the program's cancellation, many people personally blame him for consigning the Arrows to the scrapyard. The truth seems to be that Diefenbaker was indifferent to the fate of the surviving aircraft, but security and cost-recovery procedures of the time doomed the aircraft. Myths have also grown around the destruction of plans of the aircraft, although many drawings, photos and models of the Arrow survive to this day.

One contentious issue weighing heavily on the minds of the Chiefs of Staff and the Cabinet was the cost of the Arrow. In 1954, the program was estimated to cost $118 million and resulted in the building of 40 aircraft. Shortly after the program was cancelled, having completed five aircraft, the price tag stood at $247 million for the aircraft and $132 million for the Iroquois engine, a total of $379 million. Various figures were raised for the cost to build 100 Arrows: Avro quoted $3.5 million each for new aircraft, probably a lowball estimate, and Diefenbaker spoke about a $9 million cost for each Arrow, which included money already spent. Although both numbers are suspect, the fact remains that neither side had a very good track record of predicting the Arrow's costs. As well, a great deal of development needed to be done before the Arrow could be put in service, and that development work would cost money. At a time when the entire national budget stood at roughly $6 billion, the costs of the Arrow gave C.D. Howe the "shudders," and the Diefenbaker Conservatives no doubt shared this feeling. The Arrow was eating up a major part of the defence budget at a time when Canadians wanted money spent on other priorities.

Interestingly, when the controversy over the Arrow began to revive in the late 1970s, more Canadians were turning to conservative political ideas. Right-wing think tanks and watchdog groups posed questions about spending on major government projects, be they arms projects, infrastructure or industrial development programs. In the years since, conservatives and sometimes left-wing critics of certain government programs have tried to halt or derail these efforts by criticizing their cost.

In his 1989 article on the Arrow, historian Michael Bliss listed some of the more controversial high technology efforts that followed the CF-105. "In the next 30 years, Canada thus became a world leader in Canadian-designed [Candu] nuclear reactors that no one wants to buy, rusting heavy-water plants in Nova Scotia, distinctively Canadian computers (the Hyperion) and videotex systems (Telidon) for which there are no users, Bricklin automobiles in New Brunswick and hydroponic cucumbers in Newfoundland. In energy, Dome Petroleum took off to become the Avro of the 1970s. In the skies, Canadair's Challenger [executive jet] eventually cost us more than 10 times the losses on the Arrow."

Some people would contest at least parts of Bliss' list. For example, the Challenger jet has turned into a family of jet aircraft that has made Canada's Bombardier Aerospace the third or fourth largest manufacturer of passenger aircraft in the world, depending on whether sales or workforce are used as the measures, after only Boeing and Airbus, and alongside Brazil's Embraer. The Canadian government's efforts in space have built a communications satellite support and robotics industry.

And the list of Canadian high technology projects is growing, both in government and the private sector. Nortel, the Canadian communications technology company, helped lead the internet revolution in the 1990s only to leave investors wallowing in red ink following the dot-com meltdown of Internet stocks early in the new century. Controversial government-backed megaprojects include hydroelectric projects in British Columbia, Manitoba, Québec and Labrador, oil exploration off Nova Scotia and Newfoundland and in the Arctic, and plans for pipelines from the North. Three Olympic Games—Montréal in 1976, Calgary in 1988 and Vancouver in 2010—have required massive building programs and, especially in the case of Montréal, generated large deficits. Mass transit projects in Montréal, Toronto, Calgary, Edmonton and Vancouver have involved new technologies and great expense. The Québec Liberal Party used the James Bay hydro-electric project to help win an election in the 1970s and again in the 1980s, and anger over cost overruns in the Fast Cat ferry program helped drive the New Democrats from office in BC in 2001.

In the military field, Brian Mulroney's Conservatives plunged themselves into controversy in 1986 when they awarded a maintenance contract for CF-18 jets to Canadair in Montréal instead of Bristol Aerospace in Winnipeg, and later, in his government's dying days, its choice for new military helicopters was a source of contention. The new Liberal government of Jean Chrétien cancelled the deal in 1993 and set the stage for a long-running and still continuing controversy over who should supply Canada's new generation of military helicopters.

High technology projects create hopes and sometimes dash them. In today's society, where many critics are always ready with balance sheets and calculators to count up the costs of these projects, the hopes can quickly turn into political controversy and become symbols of failure, as in the cases of the Bricklin and the Newfoundland cucumbers. The Arrow, for its part, was caught between the hopes of its builders and the fears of its political creators. Military procurement programs and other government-supported high technology programs come under much harsher examination from the public today than they did in the time of the Arrow. As Bliss suggested in his article,

Diefenbaker was ahead of political trends when he cancelled the Arrow.

Regardless of Diefenbaker's culpability in the demise of the Arrow, the decision took a toll on his political standing. Despite his political talent, Diefenbaker's administrative skills had little chance to develop in the years he spent as a defence lawyer and in opposition in Parliament before he became prime minister. Many observers believe that he took too long to reach a final conclusion on the Arrow, and the angry fallout from that decision left its mark on him. A member of his Cabinet, William Hamilton, later observed: "He began to be more and more cautious until finally we came down, in the latter stages, the last year or so, to making the decisions that one was forced to make rather than making the decisions that one should make. The government began to suffer from paralysis—and it was due to the Arrow."

CHAPTER 44

Diefenbaker and Avro

At the heart of the controversies surrounding the Arrow's demise lies the federal government's relationship with Avro Canada. C.D. Howe served as the midwife who helped bring life to Avro Canada when it was created from the marriage of the success of Victory Aircraft in Malton and the know-how of the Hawker Siddeley Group in Britain. Despite Howe protégés, such as Fred Smye and Crawford Gordon, being put in charge of the enterprise, Howe became a leading critic of Avro Canada. He played a key role in ending the Jetliner program, and he made plans to end the Arrow as soon as it was politically expedient. Howe forced Avro to concentrate on the CF-100 until it had worked out its many deficiencies, and the CF-100 became Avro Canada's sole success.

Governments and aircraft contractors use various types of contracts to regulate their relationships as aircraft are being built. In the case of the Arrow, these were agreements known as cost-plus or target-price-plus-incentive contracts. In other words, the government is on the hook if costs rise. The contractor is guaranteed a certain profit level regardless of how much the program costs. Fixed-price contracts, which

force the contractor to absorb overruns, are more popular politically. But when new technologies are involved,
companies are not willing to sign such contracts
because costs are so unpredictable. "If the name of the
game is high tech, which is what the RCAF asked for,
then someone has to pay the shot," Avro's James Floyd
wrote. "There are no free lunches."

In his examination of the Arrow, James Dow wrote
that cost-plus contracts impose responsibilities on the
government to closely monitor costs and expenditures.
"The responsibility to control cost lies with the government, and in the case of the Arrow weapon system,
the government failed miserably in this duty," Dow
wrote. "It is astonishing that a project office for the
Arrow was not set up until the fall of 1957, when cost
forecasts were reaching a billion dollars." Project offices
help governments or other customers of large-scale
high technology manage costs and raise questions
about the need for changes to programs that can boost
costs. In the case of the Arrow, the project had evolved
under the Liberal administration from an airframe
program to a much larger effort that included the
development of the airframe, Iroquois engine, Astra
weapons fire-control system and the Sparrow missile.
It was only once the Conservatives took office that the
project office was formed, but the new government
took nearly another year before they reduced the program to the airframe and the engine, and by then it
was preparing the way for the program's cancellation.

While the Arrow program was setting up a project
office, an elementary requirement for management of

such a high-technology program, the U.S. government was able to manage technology and costs on larger-scale ICBM programs in the late 1950s through more sophisticated devices such as configuration control, systems management and the use of firms separate from the main contractor to manage programs in an efficient manner.

When high-technology programs overrun their budgets, as they often do, the reason is not necessarily bad management of the job but a poor estimate of what the work entails and what it will cost. The question must be asked about the Arrow: did the RCAF realistically think about costs when it drew up its specifications for the CF-105, and did Avro look realistically at costs when it took on the project? Most likely, the government and the firm did not make a proper estimate of what building an aircraft like the Arrow would cost, and the lack of control over the program worsened the Arrow's cost overruns.

Diefenbaker, his supporters, and many of the Arrow's critics direct their fire on Avro Canada. "Through the 1950s, Avro mushroomed wildly into a single-company, Canadian military-industrial complex, fuelled by taxpayers' money and the media's naive optimism," Michael Bliss wrote. "Avro had no non-Canadian customers for the Arrow. It seemed completely unable to design and make planes that could be sold to anyone at competitive prices." He and other critics also noted how Avro used public relations efforts to keep politicians supporting the project. "The venture was risky, but Avro took no risks,"

Lukasiewicz wrote. "After the Arrow was cancelled, Avro's proposals for alternative work did not envisage any financial backing by the company."

One of the most legendary events of the whole Arrow saga was the meeting between Crawford Gordon and John Diefenbaker a few days before Cabinet's decision in September 1958 to review the program and prepare the way for its cancellation. Although the meeting may not have been decisive, Gordon clearly did not help the Arrow's cause. Some have suggested that Diefenbaker's personal animus to Gordon, Smye and those associated with his old adversary C.D. Howe may have caused him to cancel the Arrow. Although Diefenbaker was known to be a ferocious political fighter who rarely forgot a slight, there is no evidence that he put an end to the Arrow out of spite directed at Gordon or Howe, just as there is no evidence that he ordered the destruction of the surviving Arrows after the cancellation. But it is likely that his lack of political friends at Avro made it easier for the prime minister and his Cabinet to make the decision to cancel.

Where the bad relationship between the company and the Conservative government did make a difference, however, was in the disposition of Avro's greatest asset—its people. Shortly after the Diefenbaker government took power, it decided to curtail production of the already successful CF-100. Avro responded with major layoffs that made the government highly uncomfortable and likely further poisoned the relationship between Avro and the government. When Diefenbaker announced the reductions to the Arrow program and foreshadowed its cancellation, Crawford Gordon and Avro chose to stand and fight for their aircraft. Communications broke down. When the government cancelled the program, the 14,528 employees of Avro and Orenda were laid off immediately, though some were called back later.

Avro management say the language of the program termination documents forced them into acting as they did. Diefenbaker, for his part, said: "What we did not anticipate—and I admit this candidly—was the sudden, immediate and precipitate action of the Avro company in dismissing everybody on the day the decision was announced. A question suggests itself—was this unjustified action taken as part of [Avro's] pressure campaign?" But despite Diefenbaker's assurances that efforts would be made to find work for the Avro workers, along with the estimated 10,000 subcontractor workers who also lost their jobs with the end of the Arrow, government work saved only Orenda Engines. The situation for Avro's employees was worsened by Crawford Gordon's failing grip on his personal life and his job, which led to his termination a few months later.

Clearly, the poor state of communications between the company and the government contributed to the loss of Avro Canada and its talented workforce. Given the relationships between C.D. Howe and the management of Avro Canada and its parent firm in England, a shutdown of the Arrow under the Liberals would likely have been less traumatic. In any event, even critics of the Arrow decried the result of the final

disastrous interaction between government and contractor. As Julius Lukasiewicz stated, "The most serious and costly consequence of the Arrow's demise in
1959 was the dispersal and mass exodus from Canada
of so much technical and managerial talent, assembled and trained at great expense in the highly skilled
business of aircraft and engine design."

CHAPTER 45

The End of the Arrow

BY THE TIME JOHN DIEFENBAKER'S Conservatives took office in 1957, the Arrow program was on life support. Although the beauty of the Arrow's sleek lines and delta wings, and its successful early test flights, dazzled many people into believing that the Arrow was a healthy and viable aircraft, it was in fact a weapons system of growing expense and unproven utility in a time when intercontinental ballistic missiles opened up the question of what the best option would be to defend Canada and the United States. Fred Smye of Avro later blamed the change of the Arrow's missile system, which caused the Canadian government and Avro to move toward developing the Arrow's main weapon and its fire control system in Canada, as the beginning of the end for the CF-105. Before that, the unavailability of off-the-shelf engines deemed suitable for the Arrow led to the development of the Iroquois engine—a technological marvel, but one that vastly increased the expense of the Arrow. The complexity of the Arrow compared to existing aircraft such as the CF-100 caused the RCAF to cut its order in half because reserve pilots couldn't fly it, which made the Arrow's economics even shakier. By its very definition as an aircraft designed for Canadian needs, the

Arrow was difficult to sell to foreign buyers. Finally, on the very day that the Arrow was revealed to the world, it literally and figuratively fell under the shadow of *Sputnik* and the ICBM that launched it, never to emerge.

On one crucial matter, the opinion of James Floyd—the man who nurtured the Arrow as Avro Canada's vice president for engineering and then stuck up for his plane in the decades that have passed since its cancellation—comes close to that of the Arrow's critics. "If the Arrow was to be cancelled at all," Floyd wrote, "the best time would have been when we saw the RCAF specification, because they had asked for the moon and for an aircraft which was so far ahead of anything else in existence that it was sure to be expensive."

Many critics say Canada was wrong to begin the program at all. Lukasiewicz wrote that the decision to proceed with the Arrow "was rooted in the unrealistic goal of achieving industrial and military self-sufficiency in military aviation." He added: "The costly experiment was rooted in a poorly conceived military strategy, which rejected a joint role for the RCAF and the U.S. Air Force in favour of a separate RCAF role in northern defence. The operational requirements that flowed from this imperative yielded specifications for an extremely complex weapon system (the Arrow) of a performance exceeding that of any aircraft then in production or under development."

Thanks to Diefenbaker's poor relationship with Avro Canada, when he pulled the plug on the Arrow,

Canada lost of much of the Avro team that had gained invaluable and hard-won experience on the CF-100 and the Jetliner. The work done after the Arrow's demise by former Avro engineers in building aircraft elsewhere in Canada and the world, and in helping the U.S. put the first humans on the Moon, underlined the quality of this lost resource.

Another contentious part of the Avro legend has it that the Arrow's demise plunged Canada's aviation industry into a death spiral. Many experts such as Larry Milberry question this idea, noting that the Arrow cancellation removed Canada from the "dead end" area of jet fighters and helped pave the way for a healthier aviation industry. Although de Havilland Canada and Canadair, followed by Bombardier, have had their share of problems, including consolidations, government ownership and large-scale subsidy by both Liberal and Conservative governments, the aviation business everywhere else in the world has undergone similar travails. Today, as Milberry points out, Canada is the world's leading builder of regional passenger jets and is a world leader in aircraft simulation and satellite technology.

For its brief lifetime, the Arrow showed that Canadians could contend with any other nation in the realm of high technology, and Canadians continue to do so, albeit in a lower-profile fashion. To those who love the Arrow, the aircraft became Canada's Excalibur, to quote the words of playwright Clinton Bomphray. But the Arrow could never have created the conditions that could have freed Canada of the embrace of its southern neighbour, because the Arrow could not have come into being without American aid. Like the great sword of the Arthurian legend, the Arrow's beauty blinded its beholders to the fact that it was built to be a weapon. And Excalibur existed in a mythical world that seems real enough to its believers, but in fact never existed.

Acronyms

CIA – Central Intelligence Agency

DDP – Department of Defence Production, Canadian government

ICBM – Intercontinental Ballistic Missile

IGY – International Geophysical Year, 1957–58

NACA – National Advisory Committee for Aeronautics, the forerunner of NASA

NAE – National Aeronautical Establishment, a branch of the NRC

NASA – National Aeronautics and Space Administration

NATO – North Atlantic Treaty Organization

NORAD – North American Air Defense Command, now known as the North American Aerospace Defense Command

NRC – National Research Council of Canada

RAE – Royal Aeronautical Establishment, England

RAF – Royal Air Force (Great Britain)

RCAF – Royal Canadian Air Force

RCMP – Royal Canadian Mounted Police

SST – Supersonic Transport aircraft

TCA – Trans-Canada Airlines, the forerunner of Air Canada

TWA – Trans-World Airlines

UN – United Nations

USAF – United States Air Force

VTOL – Vertical Takeoff and Landing

Notes on Sources

BOOKS

Campagna, Palmiro. *Storms of Controversy: The Secret Avro Arrow Files Revealed*. Toronto: Stoddart Publishing, 1992.

Diefenbaker, John G. *One Canada: The Tumultuous Years 1962 to 1967*. Toronto: Macmillan of Canada, 1977.

Dow, James. *The Arrow*. Toronto: James Lorimer & Company, 1979.

Floyd, Jim. *The Avro Canada C102 Jetliner*. Erin, ON: Boston Mills Press, 1986.

Gainor, Chris. *Arrows to the Moon: Avro's Engineers and the Space Race*. Burlington, ON: Apogee Books, 2001.

Hotson, Fred W. *De Havilland in Canada*. Toronto: Canav Books, 1999.

Milberry, Larry. *Canada's Air Force at War and Peace*. (Vol. 3) Toronto: Canav Books, 2001.

———. *Air Transport in Canada*. (Vol. 1 & 2) Toronto: Canav Books, 1997.

———. *The Avro CF-100*. Toronto: Canav Books, 1981.

Nash, Knowlton. *Kennedy and Diefenbaker: Fear and Loathing Across the Undefended Border*. Toronto: McClelland and Stewart, 1990.

Organ, Richard et al. *Avro Arrow, the Story of the Avro Arrow from its Evolution to its Extinction*. Erin, ON: Boston Mills Press, 1980.

Peden, Murray. *Fall of an Arrow*. Toronto: Stoddart Publishing, 1987.

Roy, Reginald H. *For Most Conspicuous Bravery: A Biography of Major-General George R. Pearkes, V.C., Through Two World Wars*. Vancouver: University of British Columbia Press, 1977.

Shaw, E.K. *There Never Was an Arrow*. 2nd Edition. Ottawa: Steel Rail Publishing, 1981.

Smith, Denis. *Rogue Tory: The Life and Legend of John G. Diefenbaker.* Toronto: Macfarlane Walter and Ross, 1995.

Stewart, Greig. *Arrow Through the Heart: The Life and Times of Crawford Gordon and the Avro Arrow.* Toronto: McGraw-Hill Ryerson, 1998.

Stewart, Greig. *Shutting Down the National Dream.* Scarborough, ON: McGraw-Hill Ryerson, 1988.

Stursberg, Peter. *Diefenbaker: Leadership Gained 1956–62.* Toronto: University of Toronto Press, 1975.

Whitaker, Reg and G. Marcuse. *Cold War Canada.* Toronto: University of Toronto Press, 1994.

Whitcomb, Randall. *Avro Aircraft and Cold War Aviation.* St. Catharines, ON: Vanwell Publishing, 2002.

Zuk, Bill. *Janusz Zurakowski: The Legend in the Skies.* St. Catharines, ON: Vanwell Publishing, 2004.

———. *Avrocar: Canada's Flying Saucer.* Erin, ON: Boston Mills Press, 2001.

Zuuring, Peter. *Arrow Countdown.* Kingston, ON: Arrow Alliance Press, 2001.

———. *The Arrow Scrapbook.* Dalkeith, ON: Arrow Alliance Press, 1999.

ARTICLES

Bellett, Gerry. "Ground-bound Avro Arrow arrives for Abbotsford show." *Vancouver Sun*, July 11, 1997.

Bliss, Michael. "Shutting Down the Arrow Myth." *Report on Business Magazine* 5, no. 8 (February 1989): 29.

Chaikin, Andrew. "Fallen Arrow." *Air & Space Smithsonian* (April/May 1998): 33–41.

Hodge, Trevor A. "Canada's Avro Arrow: The legend that wasn't." *The Globe and Mail*, February 9, 1990.

Isinger, Russell, and D. C. Storey. "The Plane Truth: The Avro Canada CF-105 Arrow Program," from Donald C. Storey and

R. Bruce Shepard, eds. *The Diefenbaker Legacy: Canadian Politics, Law and Society Since 1957.* Regina: Canadian Plains Research Center, 1998: 43–55.

Lukasiewicz, Julius. "Canada's Encounter with High-Speed Aeronautics." *Technology and Culture* 27, no. 2 (April 1986): 223–261.

McDougall, Harry. "Black Friday: Five Years Later." *Saturday Night,* March 1964: 13–15.

Morton, Desmond. "A revisionist perspective on the Avro Arrow." *Toronto Star,* February 20, 1959.

Reguly, Bob. "A flight of fancy: Designer, chief test pilot say CBC drama contains more fantasy than fact." *Starweek magazine,* January 11, 1997: 36.

Woodman, Jack, "Flying the Avro Arrow." Presented to the Canadian Aeronautics and Space Symposium, Winnipeg, May 16, 1978.

Young, S. "Forty Years of Work at the McDonnell Douglas Canada Ltd. Plant, Malton." *Canadian Aeronautics and Space Journal* 25, no. 2 (Second Quarter 1979): 128–132.

Documents from the National Archives of Canada:

Office of the Prime Minister, Canada, "Revision of the Canadian Air Defence Programme." September 23, 1958.

Crawford Gordon, President, A.V. Roe Canada Ltd., "Statement to Annual Meeting of Shareholders: The Arrow and Iroquois Programs." October 27, 1958.

Letter from Raymond O'Hurley, Minister of Defence Production, to John Drysdale, M.P., June 6, 1960.

Memorandum from Air Marshall Hugh Campbell to the Minister of National Defence, April 24, 1959.

Cabinet Conclusions. Various dates between October 24, 1957, and February 27, 1959.